AROUND
— the —
World
IN 80 RECIPES

Publications International, Ltd.

Pictured on the front cover *(clockwise from top left):* Irish Beef Stew *(page 60),* Chicken Fried Rice *(page 142),* Greek Salad *(page 58),* Pressure Cooker Butter Chicken *(page 148),* Peri-Peri Chicken *(page 101)* and Mole Chili *(page 30).*

Pictured on the back cover *(clockwise from top left):* Potato Pierogi *(page 68),* Shredded Beef Tacos *(page 16),* Chicken Gyoza *(page 120)* and Mushroom and Kale Slice *(page 171).*

ISBN: 978-1-63938-138-8

Manufactured in China.

8 7 6 5 4 3 2 1

Microwave Cooking: Microwave ovens vary in wattage. Use the cooking times as guidelines and check for doneness before adding more time.

WARNING: Food preparation, baking and cooking involve inherent dangers: misuse of electric products, sharp electric tools, boiling water, hot stoves, allergic reactions, foodborne illnesses and the like, pose numerous potential risks. Publications International, Ltd. (PIL) assumes no responsibility or liability for any damages you may experience as a result of following recipes, instructions, tips or advice in this publication.

While we hope this publication helps you find new ways to eat delicious foods, you may not always achieve the results desired due to variations in ingredients, cooking temperatures, typos, errors, omissions or individual cooking abilities.

Let's get social!
 @Publications_International
@PublicationsInternational
www.pilbooks.com

Contents

North America

USA

FRIED GREEN TOMATOES

⅓ cup all-purpose flour

¼ teaspoon salt

2 eggs

1 tablespoon water

½ cup panko bread crumbs

2 large green tomatoes, cut into ½-inch-thick slices

½ cup olive oil

½ cup ranch dressing

1 tablespoon sriracha sauce

1 package (5 ounces) spring greens salad mix

¼ cup crumbled goat cheese

1 Combine flour and salt in shallow bowl. Beat eggs and water in another shallow bowl. Place panko in third shallow bowl. Coat both sides of tomato slices with flour mixture, shaking off excess. Dip in egg mixture, letting excess drip back into bowl. Roll in panko to coat. Place on plate.

2 Heat oil in large skillet over medium-high heat. Add half of tomato slices, arranging in single layer in skillet. (Cook tomatoes in two batches; do not overlap in skillet.) Cook about 2 minutes per side or until golden brown. Remove to paper towel-lined plate.

3 Combine ranch dressing and sriracha in small bowl; mix well. Divide greens among four serving plates; top with tomatoes. Drizzle with dressing mixture; sprinkle with cheese.

MAKES 4 SERVINGS

TACOS WITH CARNITAS

2 pounds pork shoulder or roast, trimmed of fat

1 medium onion, quartered

3 bay leaves

2 tablespoons chili powder

1 tablespoon dried oregano

2 teaspoons salt

1 teaspoon ground cumin

Salsa Cruda (recipe follows)

16 (6-inch) corn tortillas, warmed

4 cups shredded romaine lettuce

1 cup crumbled cotija cheese, queso fresco or feta cheese

1 can (4 ounces) diced mild green chiles

1 Combine pork, onion, bay leaves, chili powder, oregano, salt and cumin in large saucepan or Dutch oven. Add enough water to cover pork. Cover; bring to a boil. Reduce heat to medium-low; simmer 3 hours or until pork is fork-tender. Meanwhile, prepare Salsa Cruda.

2 Preheat oven to 450°F. Transfer pork to large baking dish. Bake 20 minutes or until browned and crisp.

3 Meanwhile, skim fat from cooking liquid. Bring to a boil over high heat. Boil 20 minutes or until reduced to about 1 cup. Remove and discard bay leaves.

4 When cool enough to handle, shred pork with two forks. Add to saucepan; stir to coat. Cover and simmer 10 minutes or until most liquid is absorbed. Remove pork to medium bowl with slotted spoon; discard liquid.

5 Top each tortilla with ¼ cup lettuce, ¼ cup pork, 1 tablespoon cheese, 1 teaspoon chiles and 1 tablespoon Salsa Cruda.

MAKES 8 SERVINGS

Salsa Cruda

Combine 1 cup chopped tomato, 2 tablespoons minced onion, 2 tablespoons minced fresh cilantro, 2 tablespoons lime juice, ½ jalapeño pepper, seeded and minced, and 1 clove minced garlic in medium bowl; mix gently.

JAMBALAYA

1 package (16 ounces) Cajun sausage, sliced

1 cup chopped onion

1 cup chopped green bell pepper

2 cloves garlic, minced

2 cups uncooked rice

2 cups chicken broth

1 bottle (12 ounces) light-colored beer, such as pale ale

½ teaspoon salt

½ teaspoon black pepper

1 can (about 14 ounces) diced tomatoes with green pepper, onion and celery

1 teaspoon Cajun seasoning

1 pound medium cooked shrimp, peeled and deveined (with tails on)

Chopped fresh parsley and hot pepper sauce (optional)

1 Brown sausage in large saucepan or Dutch oven over medium-high heat; drain fat. Add onion, bell pepper and garlic; cook and stir 2 to 3 minutes or until tender. Add rice, broth, beer, salt and pepper; bring to a boil. Reduce heat to low; cover and simmer 20 minutes, stirring occasionally.

2 Stir in tomatoes and Cajun seasoning; cook 5 minutes. Add shrimp; cook 2 to 3 minutes or until heated through. Sprinkle with parsley and hot pepper sauce, if desired.

MAKES 6 SERVINGS

POZOLE

¼ cup plus 1 tablespoon vegetable oil, divided

3 (6-inch) corn tortillas, cut into ¼-inch-wide strips

1 large onion, chopped

1 tablespoon minced garlic

1 tablespoon dried oregano

1½ teaspoons ground cumin

2 cans (about 14 ounces each) chicken broth

1½ cups water

1 teaspoon salt

1 pound boneless skinless chicken breasts

2 cans (15 ounces each) yellow hominy, drained

1 red or green bell pepper, chopped

1 can (4 ounces) diced mild green chiles

1 can (2¼ ounces) sliced black olives, drained

½ cup lightly packed fresh cilantro, coarsely chopped

1 Heat ¼ cup oil in medium saucepan over medium-high heat. Add tortilla strips; cook and stir 3 to 4 minutes or until firm and crisp. Remove to paper towel-lined plate with tongs; set aside.

2 Heat remaining 1 tablespoon oil in large saucepan over medium heat. Add onion, garlic, oregano and cumin; cover and cook about 6 minutes or until onion is golden brown, stirring occasionally. Add broth, water and salt; cover and bring to a boil over high heat. Stir in chicken. Reduce heat to low; cover and cook 8 minutes or until chicken is no longer pink in center. Remove chicken to plate; set aside until cool enough to handle. Cut into ½-inch pieces.

3 Meanwhile, add hominy, bell pepper, chiles and olives to broth; cover and bring to a boil over medium-high heat. Reduce heat to medium-low; simmer 4 minutes or until bell pepper is crisp-tender.

4 Return chicken to saucepan. Stir in cilantro; top with tortilla strips.

MAKES 6 SERVINGS

USA

CRISPY CHICKEN SANDWICH

2 boneless skinless chicken breasts (6 to 8 ounces each)

4 cups cold water

¼ cup granulated sugar

3 tablespoons plus 1 teaspoon salt, divided

Peanut or vegetable oil for frying

1 cup milk

2 eggs

1½ cups all-purpose flour

2 tablespoons powdered sugar

2 teaspoons paprika

2 teaspoons black pepper

¾ teaspoon baking powder

½ teaspoon ground red pepper

8 dill pickle slices

4 soft hamburger buns, toasted and buttered

1 Pound chicken to ½-inch thickness between two sheets of waxed paper or plastic wrap with rolling pin or meat mallet. Cut each breast in half crosswise to create total of four pieces.

2 Combine water, granulated sugar and 3 tablespoons salt in medium bowl; stir until sugar and salt are dissolved. Add chicken to brine; cover and refrigerate 2 to 4 hours. Remove chicken from refrigerator about 30 minutes before cooking.

3 Heat at least 3 inches of oil in large saucepan over medium-high heat to 350°F; adjust heat to maintain temperature. Meanwhile, beat milk and eggs in medium shallow dish until blended. Combine flour, powdered sugar, paprika, black pepper, remaining 1 teaspoon salt, baking powder and red pepper in another shallow dish; mix well.

4 Working with one piece at a time, remove chicken from brine and add to egg mixture, turning to coat. Place in flour mixture; turn to coat completely and shake off excess. Lower chicken gently into hot oil; fry 6 to 8 minutes or until cooked through (165°F) and crust is golden brown and crisp, turning occasionally. Drain on paper towel-lined plate.

5 Place 2 pickle slices on bottom halves of buns; top with chicken and top halves of buns. Serve immediately.

MAKES 4 SERVINGS

NEW ENGLAND BAKED BEANS

4 slices bacon, chopped

3 cans (about 15 ounces each) Great Northern beans, rinsed and drained

1 onion, chopped

¾ cup water

⅓ cup canned diced tomatoes, well drained

3 tablespoons packed brown sugar

3 tablespoons maple syrup

3 tablespoons molasses

2 cloves garlic, minced

½ teaspoon salt

½ teaspoon dry mustard

⅛ teaspoon black pepper

½ bay leaf

Slow Cooker Directions

1 Cook bacon in large skillet over medium-high heat until almost chewy but not crisp. Drain on paper towel-lined plate. Remove to slow cooker.

2 Add beans, onion, water, tomatoes, brown sugar, maple syrup, molasses, garlic, salt, mustard, pepper and bay leaf to slow cooker; mix well.

3 Cover; cook on LOW 6 to 8 hours or until thickened. Remove and discard bay leaf.

MAKES 4 TO 6 SERVINGS

 MEXICO

SHREDDED BEEF TACOS

1 boneless beef chuck roast
  (2½ pounds)

1¼ teaspoons salt, divided

1 teaspoon *each* ground
  cumin, garlic powder
  and smoked paprika

2 tablespoons olive oil,
  divided

2 cups beef broth

1 red bell pepper, sliced

1 tomato, cut into wedges

½ onion, sliced

2 cloves garlic, minced

1 to 2 canned chipotle
  peppers in adobo sauce

Juice of 1 lime

Corn or flour tortillas

Optional toppings: sliced
  bell peppers, avocado,
  diced onion, lime
  wedges and/or chopped
  fresh cilantro

Slow Cooker Directions

1 Season beef with 1 teaspoon salt, cumin, garlic powder and smoked paprika. Heat 1 tablespoon oil in large skillet over medium-high heat. Add beef; cook 5 minutes per side or until browned. Remove to slow cooker. Pour in broth.

2 Cover; cook on LOW 8 to 9 hours or on HIGH 4 to 5 hours.

3 Meanwhile, preheat oven to 425°F. Combine bell pepper, tomato, onion and garlic on large baking sheet. Drizzle with remaining 1 tablespoon oil. Roast 40 minutes or until vegetables are tender.

4 Combine vegetables, chipotle pepper, lime juice and remaining ¼ teaspoon salt in food processor or blender; blend until smooth.

5 Remove beef to large cutting board; shred with two forks. Combine shredded meat with 1 cup cooking liquid. Discard remaining cooking liquid. Serve meat on tortillas with sauce and desired toppings.

MAKES 6 TO 8 SERVINGS

USA

FRIED CATFISH
WITH HUSH PUPPIES

2 cups yellow cornmeal, divided

½ cup plus 3 tablespoons all-purpose flour, divided

2 teaspoons baking powder

2 teaspoons salt, divided

1 cup milk

1 small onion, minced

1 egg, lightly beaten

Vegetable oil for frying

¼ teaspoon ground red pepper

4 catfish fillets (about 6 ounces each)

1 Combine 1½ cups cornmeal, ½ cup flour, baking powder and ½ teaspoon salt in medium bowl. Stir in milk, onion and egg until well blended. Let stand 5 to 10 minutes before frying.

2 Heat 2 inches of oil in large saucepan over medium-high heat to 375°F; adjust heat to maintain temperature. Combine remaining ½ cup cornmeal, 3 tablespoons flour, 1½ teaspoons salt and red pepper in shallow dish. Coat fish with cornmeal mixture.

3 Fry fish in batches 4 to 5 minutes or until golden brown and fish begins to flake when tested with fork. Drain fish on paper towel-lined plate.

4 For hush puppies, drop batter by tablespoonfuls into hot oil. Fry in batches 2 minutes or until golden brown. Drain on paper towel-lined plate.

MAKES 4 SERVINGS

TWO–CHEESE BURGERS

1½ pounds ground beef

⅓ cup chopped fresh parsley

1 tablespoon Dijon mustard

1 tablespoon Worcestershire sauce

¾ teaspoon black pepper, divided

½ teaspoon dried thyme

½ thinly sliced English cucumber

3 slices red onion, separated into rings

4 radishes, thinly sliced

1 tablespoon olive oil

1 teaspoon red wine vinegar

¼ teaspoon salt

4 slices Cheddar cheese

4 slices Gouda cheese

4 leaves green leaf lettuce

4 whole wheat rolls, split and toasted

Ketchup

1 Prepare grill for direct cooking. Combine beef, parsley, mustard, Worcestershire sauce, ½ teaspoon pepper and thyme in large bowl; mix gently. Shape into four patties about ¾ inch thick. Cover and refrigerate.

2 Combine cucumber, onion, radishes, oil, vinegar, salt and remaining ¼ teaspoon pepper in small bowl; mix well.

3 Grill patties, covered, over medium heat 8 to 10 minutes (or uncovered 13 to 15 minutes) to medium (160°F) or to desired doneness, turning halfway through grilling time. Top burgers with Cheddar during last 2 minutes of grilling.

4 Place Gouda slice on bottom half of each roll; top with cucumber mixture, lettuce and burgers. Spread ketchup on top half of each roll; place on burgers.

MAKES 4 SERVINGS

 MEXICO

PRESSURE COOKER TACOS AL PASTOR

1 medium pineapple

1 small red onion, coarsely chopped

Juice of 1 orange

Juice of 1 lime

2 canned chipotle peppers in adobo sauce

1 tablespoon white vinegar

1 tablespoon chili powder

2 teaspoons salt

2 cloves garlic

1 teaspoon ground cumin

½ teaspoon black pepper

2½ pounds boneless pork shoulder, cut into 2-inch pieces

Flour or corn tortillas, heated

Optional toppings: pickled red onion, chopped fresh cilantro, diced avocado and/or lime wedges

1 Peel and core pineapple; set aside half for topping. Coarsely chop remaining half; place in food processor with onion, orange juice, lime juice, chipotle peppers, vinegar, chili powder, salt, garlic, cumin and black pepper. Process until smooth.

2 Place pork in large resealable food storage bag; pour marinade over pork. Seal bag and turn to coat. Marinate in refrigerator at least 4 hours or overnight.

3 Pour pork and marinade into pot of electric pressure cooker. Secure lid and move pressure release valve to sealing or locked position. Cook at high pressure 40 minutes.

4 Meanwhile, cut reserved half of pineapple into ½-inch pieces. Preheat broiler. Line baking sheet with foil. Spread pineapple on one third of baking sheet.

5 When cooking is complete, use natural release for 10 minutes, then release remaining pressure. Remove pork to prepared baking sheet; break into smaller chunks and spread out next to pineapple. Broil 5 to 8 minutes or until pork and pineapple begin to brown and char in spots.

6 Meanwhile, press Sauté; cook liquid in pot 5 to 10 minutes or until reduced and thickened slightly. Drizzle sauce over pork; serve pork and pineapple in tortillas with desired toppings.

MAKES 6 TO 8 SERVINGS

NEW ORLEANS–STYLE MUFFALETTA

¾ cup pitted green olives

½ cup pitted kalamata olives

½ cup giardiniera
(Italian-style pickled
vegetables), drained

2 tablespoons fresh parsley
leaves

2 tablespoons capers

1 clove garlic, minced

2 tablespoons olive oil

1 tablespoon red wine
vinegar

1 (8-inch) round Italian loaf
(16 to 22 ounces)

8 ounces thinly sliced ham

8 ounces thinly sliced
Genoa salami

6 ounces thinly sliced
provolone cheese

1 Combine olives, giardiniera, parsley, capers and garlic in food processor; pulse until coarsely chopped and no large pieces remain. Transfer to small bowl; stir in oil and vinegar until well blended. Cover and refrigerate several hours or overnight to blend flavors.

2 Cut bread in half crosswise. Spread two thirds of olive salad over bottom half of bread; layer with ham, salami and cheese. Spread remaining olive salad over cheese; top with top half of bread, pressing down slightly to compress. Wrap sandwich with plastic wrap; let stand 1 hour to blend flavors.

3 To serve sandwich warm, preheat oven to 350°F. Remove plastic wrap; wrap sandwich loosely in foil. Bake 5 to 10 minutes or just until sandwich is slightly warm and cheese begins to melt. Cut into wedges.

MAKES 4 TO 6 SERVINGS

CHILE RELLENOS

6 whole poblano peppers

2½ cups (10 ounces) grated Chihuahua cheese or queso fresco, divided

½ cup plus 2 tablespoons prepared salsa verde, divided

¼ cup plus 2 tablespoons fresh cilantro leaves, divided

1 (1-inch) piece fresh serrano pepper

1 large clove garlic

1 can (12 ounces) evaporated milk

2 tablespoons all-purpose flour

2 eggs

⅔ cup sour cream

Slow Cooker Directions

1 Spray inside of slow cooker with nonstick cooking spray. Preheat broiler. Place poblano peppers on baking sheet; broil about 4 inches from heat just until skins blister, turning occasionally. Place in paper bag or resealable food storage bag. Close bag; let stand 5 minutes. Scrape skin from peppers. Cut down one side of each pepper; open flat and remove any seeds or membranes. Pat dry with paper towels.

2 Divide 1½ cups cheese evenly among poblano peppers; roll to enclose. Arrange poblano peppers in single layer in bottom of slow cooker.

3 Combine ½ cup salsa verde, ¼ cup cilantro, serrano pepper and garlic in food processor or blender; pulse to blend. Add evaporated milk, flour and eggs; process until smooth. Pour salsa mixture over poblano peppers; top with remaining 1 cup cheese.

4 Cover; cook on LOW 3 hours. Meanwhile, combine sour cream and remaining 2 tablespoons salsa verde in small bowl; stir to blend. Refrigerate until ready to serve.

5 If desired, remove poblano peppers from slow cooker to large baking sheet. Preheat broiler. Broil 3 to 5 minutes or until browned. Garnish with sour cream mixture and remaining 2 tablespoons cilantro.

MAKES 6 SERVINGS

SWEET SOUTHERN BARBECUE CHICKEN

2 to 3 tablespoons olive oil, divided

½ cup chopped onion

1 clove garlic, minced

½ cup packed brown sugar

1 teaspoon dry mustard

1 tablespoon honey mustard

1 tablespoon Dijon mustard

1 cup cola beverage

2 tablespoons balsamic vinegar

2 tablespoons cider vinegar

2 tablespoons Worcestershire sauce

½ cup ketchup

2 to 3 pounds boneless skinless chicken thighs

1 Heat 1 tablespoon oil in medium skillet over medium heat. Add onion and garlic; cook and stir 2 minutes. Add brown sugar and mustards; bring to a boil over medium-high heat. Reduce heat to low; simmer 20 minutes or until sauce thickens.

2 Stir in cola, balsamic vinegar, cider vinegar, Worcestershire sauce and ketchup; simmer 15 to 20 minutes or until sauce thickens. Remove from heat.

3 Heat 1 tablespoon oil in large skillet over medium-high heat. Add half of chicken; cook 5 to 7 minutes. Turn and brush with sauce; cook 5 to 7 minutes or until cooked through. Brush both sides of chicken with sauce during last 1 to 2 minutes of cooking. Remove to plate; keep warm. Repeat with remaining oil, sauce and chicken. Serve with additional sauce.

MAKES 4 SERVINGS

 MEXICO

MOLE CHILI

2 corn tortillas, each cut into 4 wedges

1½ pounds boneless beef chuck, cut into 1-inch pieces

¾ teaspoon salt

½ teaspoon black pepper

3 tablespoons olive oil, divided

2 medium onions, chopped

5 cloves garlic, minced

1 cup beef broth

1 can (about 14 ounces) fire-roasted diced tomatoes

2 tablespoons chili powder

1 tablespoon ground ancho chile

1 teaspoon ground cumin

1 teaspoon dried oregano

¾ teaspoon ground cinnamon

1 can (about 15 ounces) red kidney beans, rinsed and drained

1½ ounces semisweet chocolate, chopped

Queso fresco and chopped fresh cilantro (optional)

Slow Cooker Directions

1 Spray inside of slow cooker with nonstick cooking spray. Place tortillas in food processor or blender; process to fine crumbs. Set aside.

2 Season beef with salt and pepper. Heat 1 tablespoon oil in large skillet over medium-high heat. Add half of beef; cook 4 minutes or until browned. Remove to slow cooker. Repeat with 1 tablespoon oil and remaining beef.

3 Heat remaining 1 tablespoon oil in same skillet. Add onions and garlic; cook and stir 2 minutes or until onions begin to soften. Stir in broth, scraping up browned bits from bottom of skillet. Remove to slow cooker. Stir in tortilla crumbs, tomatoes, chili powder, ancho chile, cumin, oregano and cinnamon.

4 Cover; cook on LOW 8 to 8½ hours. Stir in beans. Cover; cook on LOW 30 minutes. Turn off heat. Add chocolate; stir until chocolate is melted. Top with queso fresco and cilantro, if desired.

MAKES 4 TO 6 SERVINGS

CANADA

MAPLE WALNUT COOKIES

Cookies

- ¾ cup (1½ sticks) butter, softened
- ¾ cup granulated sugar
- 3 egg yolks
- 1 teaspoon maple extract
- 2 cups all-purpose flour
- ¾ cup finely chopped walnuts
- ¼ teaspoon salt
- ¾ cup finely chopped walnuts

Icing

- 2½ cups powdered sugar
- 3 teaspoons maple extract

1 Beat butter and granulated sugar in large bowl with electric mixer at medium speed 1 minute. Beat in egg yolks and 1 teaspoon maple extract until well blended. Add flour, walnuts and salt; beat at low speed just until blended.

2 Divide dough in half. Shape into 2 rectangular 6×3×1-inch blocks. Wrap each block in plastic wrap. Refrigerate at least 2 hours or overnight.

3 Preheat oven to 375°F. Line cookie sheets with parchment paper. Unwrap dough; cut blocks into 3×¼-inch slices. Place cookies 1-inch apart on baking sheets.

4 Bake 12 to 14 minutes or until edges are lightly browned. Cool on cookie sheets 5 minutes. Remove to wire racks; cool completely.

5 For icing, whisk powdered sugar and 3 teaspoons maple extract in small deep bowl until smooth. Dip half of each cookie into icing. Place iced cookies on parchment or waxed paper; let stand until icing is firm.

MAKES 3½ DOZEN COOKIES

ST. LOUIS GOOEY BUTTER CAKE

1 package (about 15 ounces) yellow cake mix *without* pudding in the mix

½ cup (1 stick) butter, melted

4 eggs, divided

1 package (8 ounces) cream cheese, softened

1 teaspoon vanilla

3 cups powdered sugar, plus additional for topping

1 Preheat oven to 350°F. Spray 13×9-inch baking pan with nonstick cooking spray.

2 Beat cake mix, butter and 2 eggs in large bowl with electric mixer at low speed 1 minute or just until blended. Press mixture evenly into bottom of prepared pan.

3 Beat cream cheese, remaining 2 eggs and vanilla in medium bowl with electric mixer at medium-high speed 1 minute or until well blended. Slowly add 3 cups powdered sugar; beat until smooth. Spread evenly over cake mix layer in pan.

4 Bake 35 to 40 minutes or until top is lightly browned. (Cake will puff up then collapse during baking to make gooey center.) Cool completely in pan on wire rack. Sprinkle with additional powdered sugar, if desired.

MAKES 12 TO 15 SERVINGS

CLASSIC FLAN

1½ cups sugar, divided

1 tablespoon water

¼ teaspoon ground cinnamon

3 cups whole milk

3 eggs

3 egg yolks

1 teaspoon vanilla

1 Preheat oven to 300°F.

2 Combine 1 cup sugar, water and cinnamon in medium saucepan; cook over medium-high heat without stirring about 10 minutes or until sugar is melted and mixture is deep golden amber in color. Pour into six 6-ounce ramekins, swirling to coat bottoms. Place ramekins in 13×9-inch baking pan.

3 Heat milk in separate medium saucepan over medium heat until bubbles begin to form around edge of pan.

4 Meanwhile, whisk eggs, egg yolks, vanilla and remaining ½ cup sugar in medium bowl until well blended. Whisk in ½ cup hot milk in thin, steady stream. Gradually whisk in remaining milk. Divide milk mixture evenly among ramekins. Carefully add hot water to baking pan until water comes halfway up sides of ramekins. Cover ramekins with waxed paper or parchment paper.

5 Bake 1 hour 15 minutes or until custard is firm and knife inserted into custard comes out clean. Remove ramekins from baking pan to wire rack; cool completely. Cover and refrigerate until cold. Run small knife around edges of ramekins; invert flan onto serving plates.

MAKES 6 SERVINGS

ALL–AMERICAN APPLE PIE

- 1 package (15 ounces) refrigerated pie crusts (2 crusts) or Double Crust Pie Pastry (recipe follows)
- 6 cups sliced Granny Smith, Honeycrisp or Fuji apples (about 6 medium)
- ½ cup sugar
- 1 tablespoon cornstarch
- 2 teaspoons lemon juice
- ½ teaspoon ground cinnamon
- ½ teaspoon vanilla
- ⅛ teaspoon salt
- ⅛ teaspoon ground nutmeg
- ⅛ teaspoon ground cloves
- 1 tablespoon whipping cream

1 Let one crust stand at room temperature 15 minutes. Preheat oven to 350°F. Line deep-dish 9-inch pie plate with crust.

2 Combine apples, sugar, cornstarch, lemon juice, cinnamon, vanilla, salt, nutmeg and cloves in large bowl; toss to coat. Pour into crust. Place second crust over apples; crimp edge to seal. Cut four slits in top crust; brush with cream.

3 Bake 40 minutes or until crust is golden brown. Cool completely on wire rack.

MAKES 8 SERVINGS

Double Crust Pie Pastry

Combine 2½ cups all-purpose flour, 1 teaspoon granulated sugar and 1 teaspoon salt in large bowl. Cut in 1 cup (2 sticks) cold cubed unsalted butter with pastry blender or fingertips until coarse crumbs form. Combine 7 tablespoons ice water and 1 tablespoon cider vinegar in small bowl. Drizzle in just enough water mixture until dough begins to come together, stirring with fork. Turn out dough onto lightly floured surface; press into a ball. Divide in half. Shape each half into a disc; wrap with plastic wrap. Refrigerate at least 30 minutes.

South America

ARGENTINA

GRILLED CHICKEN WITH CHIMICHURRI

4 boneless skinless chicken breasts (6 ounces each)

½ cup plus 4 teaspoons olive oil, divided

Salt and black pepper

½ cup finely chopped fresh parsley

¼ cup white wine vinegar

2 tablespoons finely chopped onion

3 cloves garlic, minced

1 jalapeño pepper, finely chopped

2 teaspoons dried oregano

1 Prepare grill for direct cooking.

2 Brush chicken with 4 teaspoons oil; season with salt and black pepper. Grill chicken, covered, over medium heat 5 to 7 minutes per side or until no longer pink in center (165°F).

3 For chimichurri, combine parsley, remaining ½ cup oil, vinegar, onion, garlic, jalapeño pepper and oregano in small bowl. Season with salt and black pepper. Serve over chicken.

MAKES 4 SERVINGS

 BRAZIL

BRAZILIAN CHEESE ROLLS
(PÃO DE QUEIJO)

1 cup whole milk

¼ cup (½ stick) butter, cut into pieces

¼ cup vegetable oil

2 cups plus 2 tablespoons tapioca flour*

2 eggs

1 cup grated Parmesan cheese or other firm cheese

Sometimes labeled tapioca starch.

1 Preheat oven to 350°F.

2 Combine milk, butter and oil in large saucepan; heat to a boil over medium heat, stirring to melt butter. Once mixture reaches a boil, remove from heat; stir in tapioca flour. Mixture will be thick and stretchy.

3 Stir in eggs, one at a time, and cheese. Mixture will be very stiff. Cool mixture in pan until easy to handle.

4 Use tapioca-floured hands to roll heaping tablespoons of dough into 1½-inch balls. Place about 1 inch apart on ungreased baking sheet.

5 Bake 20 to 25 minutes or until puffed and golden. Serve warm.

MAKES ABOUT 20 ROLLS

Note

These moist, chewy rolls are a Brazilian specialty and are always made with tapioca flour instead of wheat flour (so they are naturally gluten-free). In Brazil they are popular at breakfast, lunch or dinner.

COLOMBIA

AREPAS
(LATIN AMERICAN CORN CAKES)

1½ cups instant corn flour
for arepas*

½ teaspoon salt

1½ to 2 cups hot water

⅓ cup shredded Mexican
cheese blend

1 tablespoon butter, melted

*This flour is also called
masarepa, masa al instante and
harina precodica. It is not the
same as masa harina or regular
cornmeal. Purchase arepa flour
at Latin American markets or
online.*

1 Preheat oven to 350°F. Combine instant corn flour and salt in medium bowl. Stir in 1½ cups hot water until blended. Dough should be smooth and moist but not sticky; add additional water, 1 tablespoon at a time, if necessary. Add cheese and butter; knead until dough is consistency of smooth mashed potatoes.

2 Lightly grease heavy skillet or griddle; heat over medium heat. Divide dough into six to eight equal pieces; flatten and pat dough into 4-inch discs about ½ inch thick. (If dough cracks or is too dry, return to bowl and add additional water, 1 tablespoon at a time.)

3 Immediately place dough pieces in hot skillet. Cook 3 to 5 minutes per side or until browned in spots. Remove to baking sheet.

4 Bake 15 minutes or until arepas sound hollow when tapped. Serve warm.

5 If desired, make breakfast sandwiches by splitting arepas with fork as you would English muffins. Fill with eggs, cheese and salsa as desired.

MAKES 6 TO 8 AREPAS

Tip

Freeze leftover arepas in airtight freezer food storage bags.

SOUTH AMERICAN
CHICKEN AND QUINOA

Tomato-Apricot Chutney
  (page 47)
1 teaspoon ground turmeric
1 teaspoon dried thyme
¾ teaspoon salt, divided
1 pound boneless skinless
  chicken breasts, cut
  into 1-inch pieces
2 tablespoons olive oil,
  divided
1 large red or green bell
  pepper, chopped
1 medium onion, chopped
1 cup uncooked quinoa
1 cup chicken broth
1 cup unsweetened
  coconut milk
1 teaspoon curry powder
¼ teaspoon ground ginger

1 Prepare Tomato-Apricot Chutney; set aside.

2 Combine turmeric, thyme and ¼ teaspoon salt in shallow dish. Add chicken; toss to coat.

3 Heat 1 tablespoon oil in large skillet over medium-high heat. Add bell pepper and onion; cook and stir 2 minutes or until vegetables are crisp-tender. Remove to medium bowl.

4 Add remaining 1 tablespoon oil to skillet. Add chicken; cook and stir 5 minutes or until golden brown and cooked through.

5 Place quinoa in fine-mesh strainer; rinse well under cold water. Combine quinoa, broth, coconut milk, curry powder, remaining ½ teaspoon salt and ginger in large saucepan; bring to a boil over high heat. Reduce heat to low; cover and simmer 10 minutes.

6 Stir chicken and pepper mixture into quinoa; cook 5 minutes or until liquid is absorbed and quinoa is tender. Serve with Tomato-Apricot Chutney.

MAKES 4 SERVINGS

TOMATO-APRICOT CHUTNEY

¾ cup apple cider or juice

¾ cup finely diced dried apricots

½ cup currants or golden raisins

3 tablespoons cider vinegar

1 can (about 14 ounces) diced tomatoes, drained

1 tablespoon packed dark brown sugar

1 teaspoon ground ginger

⅛ teaspoon ground cloves

1 Combine apple cider, apricots, currants and vinegar in small saucepan; bring to a boil over high heat. Reduce heat to low; cover and simmer 10 minutes.

2 Stir in tomatoes, brown sugar, ginger and cloves; simmer, uncovered, 5 minutes or until liquid is absorbed.

FEIJOADA COMPLETA

1½ pounds (3 cups) dried
  black beans

 1 corned beef brisket
  (3 to 4 pounds)

 2 pounds pork spareribs
  or country-style ribs

 ¼ pound piece Canadian
  bacon *or* 1 meaty
  ham hock

  Chili-Lemon Sauce
  (page 49)

1½ pounds smoked link
  sausage, such as
  Polish or andouille

1½ pounds fresh link sausage,
  such as bratwurst or
  breakfast links

 2 medium onions, chopped

 6 cloves garlic, minced

 2 jalapeño peppers,
  seeded and chopped

 2 tablespoons vegetable oil

 3 tablespoons butter

 3 pounds fresh kale, rinsed,
  drained, stemmed and
  cut into 3- to 4-inch
  pieces

 1 large ripe tomato,
  chopped

 2 tablespoons chopped
  fresh parsley

 6 to 8 cups hot cooked rice

1 Rinse beans well in colander under cold water, picking out any debris or blemished beans. Combine beans, corned beef, spareribs, Canadian bacon and 4 quarts water in large stockpot; bring to a boil over high heat. Reduce heat to medium-low; cover and simmer 2 to 3 hours or until beans and meat are very tender.

2 Meanwhile, prepare Chili-Lemon Sauce.

3 Add sausages to bean mixture; cook about 15 minutes or until heated through. Remove corned beef, spareribs, Canadian bacon and sausages to cutting board. Slice corned beef; place in center of large serving platter. Cut remaining meat into cubes and arrange around corned beef. Cover meat and keep warm in 200°F oven.

4 Drain liquid from beans, reserving 1 cup liquid. Combine onions, garlic, jalapeño peppers and oil in large skillet; cook and stir over medium-high heat 6 minutes or until onions are tender. Remove from heat. Add 2 cups beans to onion mixture; mash with potato masher or fork. Add remaining beans and reserved 1 cup liquid; simmer 10 to 15 minutes.

5 Melt 1 tablespoon butter with 2 tablespoons water in Dutch oven over medium-high heat. Add about one third of kale; cook and stir 1 minute. Cover and steam kale 3 to 5 minutes or until kale is wilted and tender but not soft, stirring occasionally. Remove to large bowl; cover to keep warm. Repeat with remaining kale, butter and additional water.

6 Transfer beans to large serving bowl; sprinkle with tomato and parsley. Serve with meat, kale, Chili-Lemon Sauce and rice.

MAKES 10 TO 12 SERVINGS

CHILI–LEMON SAUCE

¾ cup lemon juice

1 small onion, coarsely chopped

3 jalapeño peppers, stemmed, seeded and quartered

3 cloves garlic, halved

Combine all ingredients in food processor; process until smooth. Serve at room temperature.

MAKES ABOUT 1 CUP

BOLIVIAN ALMOND COOKIES (ALFAJORES DE ALMENDRAS)

- 4 cups whole natural almonds
- 1 cup all-purpose flour
- ¼ teaspoon salt
- 1 cup sugar
- ¾ cup (1½ sticks) butter, softened
- 1 teaspoon vanilla
- ½ teaspoon almond extract
- 2 eggs
- 2 tablespoons milk
- 1 tablespoon grated lemon peel
- 1 cup sliced natural almonds

1 Place 4 cups almonds in food processor; pulse until almonds are ground, but not pasty.

2 Preheat oven to 350°F. Line cookie sheets with parchment paper or lightly grease.

3 Combine ground almonds, flour and salt in medium bowl.

4 Beat sugar, butter, vanilla and almond extract in large bowl with electric mixer at medium speed until light and fluffy. Beat in eggs and milk. Gradually add half of flour mixture. Beat at low speed until well blended. Stir in lemon peel and remaining flour mixture.

5 Drop rounded teaspoonfuls of dough 2 inches apart onto prepared cookie sheets. Flatten slightly with spoon; top with sliced almonds.

6 Bake 10 to 12 minutes or until edges are lightly browned. Remove cookies to wire racks; cool completely.

MAKES ABOUT 3 DOZEN COOKIES

ARGENTINEAN CARAMEL–FILLED CRESCENTS (PASTELES)

3 cups all-purpose flour

½ cup powdered sugar

1 teaspoon baking powder

¼ teaspoon salt

1 cup (2 sticks) cold butter, cut into small pieces

6 to 7 tablespoons ice water

7 ounces caramel candies (half of 14-ounce package)

2 tablespoons milk

½ cup flaked coconut

1 egg

1 tablespoon water

1 Combine flour, powdered sugar, baking powder and salt in large bowl; stir to combine. Cut in butter with pastry blender or fingertips until mixture forms pea-sized pieces. Add water, 1 tablespoon at a time; toss with fork until mixture holds together. Divide dough in half; cover and refrigerate 30 minutes or until firm.

2 Meanwhile, melt caramels and milk in medium saucepan over low heat, stirring constantly. Stir in coconut. Remove from heat; set aside to cool.

3 Working with one portion at a time, roll out dough to ⅛-inch thickness on lightly floured surface. Cut dough with 3-inch round cookie cutter. Reroll trimmings and cut out additional cookies.

4 Preheat oven to 400°F. Line cookie sheets with parchment paper. Beat egg and water in small bowl. Place ½ teaspoon caramel mixture in center of each dough round. Moisten edge of dough round with egg mixture. Fold dough in half; press edges firmly to seal in filling. Press edges with fork. Place crescents on prepared cookie sheets; brush with egg mixture. Cut three slashes across top of each cookie with tip of knife.

5 Bake 15 to 20 minutes or until golden brown. Remove cookies to wire racks; cool completely. Store tightly covered at room temperature.

MAKES ABOUT 4 DOZEN COOKIES

Europe

GERMANY

WIENER SCHNITZEL

½ cup all-purpose flour

½ teaspoon salt

¼ teaspoon black pepper

2 eggs, beaten

¾ cup dry seasoned
   bread crumbs

4 slices veal scallopini
   (about 4 ounces each)

2 tablespoons butter

1 tablespoon olive oil

1 cup brown ale

2 tablespoons capers,
   drained

1 lemon, quartered
   (optional)

1 Combine flour, salt and pepper in shallow dish; mix well. Place eggs and bread crumbs in separate shallow dishes. Pat veal dry with paper towels. Coat each slice in flour mixture, dip into eggs and then into bread crumbs.

2 Heat butter and oil in large skillet over medium-high heat. Add veal and cook 3 to 4 minutes or until cooked through, turning once. Remove to plate; tent with foil to keep warm.

3 Add ale to skillet; bring to a boil, scraping up browned bits from bottom of skillet. Cook until slightly thickened; stir in capers. Spoon sauce over veal. Garnish with lemon wedges.

MAKES 4 SERVINGS

PAELLA

6 cups chicken broth

3 tablespoons olive oil

8 ounces boneless skinless chicken thighs, cut into bite-size pieces

2 to 3 links Spanish chorizo sausage (about 5 ounces), sliced

1 medium onion, chopped

1 red bell pepper, chopped

4 cloves garlic, minced

1 teaspoon crushed saffron threads

1½ cups uncooked rice

1 can (10 ounces) diced tomatoes with chiles

3 tablespoons tomato paste

½ teaspoon salt

¼ teaspoon black pepper

1 pound large raw shrimp, peeled and deveined (with tails on)

8 ounces mussels, scrubbed and debearded

½ cup frozen peas, thawed

1 Heat broth in medium saucepan over high heat to a boil; keep warm over low heat.

2 Heat oil in large skillet over medium-high heat. Add chicken and chorizo; cook 1 minute, stirring once. Add onion, bell pepper, garlic and saffron; cook and stir 5 minutes or until vegetables are soft and chorizo is browned.

3 Add rice, tomatoes, tomato paste, salt and black pepper; cook 5 minutes, stirring occasionally. Add broth, ½ to 1 cup at a time, stirring after each addition until broth is almost absorbed.

4 Cover skillet with foil or lid; cook over medium heat 25 to 30 minutes or until rice is tender.

5 Remove foil; gently stir in shrimp, mussels and peas. Replace foil; cook 5 to 10 minutes or until shrimp are pink and opaque and mussels open. Discard any unopened mussels.

MAKES 8 SERVINGS

GREEK SALAD

Salad

- 3 medium tomatoes, cut into 8 wedges each and seeds removed
- 1 green bell pepper, cut into 1-inch pieces
- ½ English cucumber (8 to 10 inches), quartered lengthwise and sliced crosswise
- ½ red onion, thinly sliced
- ½ cup pitted kalamata olives
- 1 block (8 ounces) feta cheese, cut into ½-inch cubes

Dressing

- 6 tablespoons extra virgin olive oil
- 3 tablespoons red wine vinegar
- 1 to 2 cloves garlic, minced
- ¾ teaspoon dried oregano
- ¾ teaspoon salt
- ¼ teaspoon black pepper

1 For salad, combine tomatoes, bell pepper, cucumber, onion and olives in large bowl. Top with cheese.

2 For dressing, whisk oil, vinegar, garlic, oregano, salt and black pepper in small bowl until well blended. Pour over salad; stir gently to coat.

MAKES 6 SERVINGS

 *Europe*

IRISH BEEF STEW

2½ tablespoons vegetable oil, divided

2 pounds boneless beef chuck roast, cut into 1-inch pieces

1½ teaspoons salt, divided

¾ teaspoon black pepper, divided

1 medium onion, chopped

3 medium carrots, cut into 1-inch pieces

3 medium parsnips, cut into 1-inch pieces

1 package (8 to 10 ounces) cremini mushrooms, quartered

2 cloves garlic, minced

1 teaspoon dried thyme

1 teaspoon dried rosemary

2 bay leaves

1 can (about 15 ounces) Guinness stout

1 can (about 14 ounces) beef broth

1 tablespoon Dijon mustard

1 tablespoon tomato paste

1 tablespoon Worcestershire sauce

1 pound small yellow potatoes (about 1¼ inches), halved

1 cup frozen pearl onions

2 teaspoons water

2 teaspoons cornstarch

Chopped fresh parsley (optional)

1 Heat 2 tablespoons oil in Dutch oven or large saucepan over medium-high heat. Season beef with 1 teaspoon salt and ½ teaspoon pepper. Cook beef in two batches 5 minutes or until browned. Remove to plate.

2 Add remaining ½ tablespoon oil and chopped onion to Dutch oven; cook and stir 3 minutes or until softened. Add carrots, parsnips and mushrooms; cook 8 minutes or until vegetables soften and mushrooms release their liquid, stirring occasionally. Add garlic, thyme, rosemary, bay leaves, remaining ½ teaspoon salt and ¼ teaspoon pepper; cook and stir 2 minutes. Add Guinness, broth, mustard, tomato paste and Worcestershire sauce; bring to a boil, scraping up browned bits from bottom of Dutch oven. Return beef and any accumulated juices to Dutch oven; mix well.

3 Reduce heat to low; cover and simmer 1 hour 30 minutes. Stir in potatoes; cover and simmer 30 minutes. Stir in pearl onions; simmer, uncovered, 30 minutes or until beef and potatoes are fork-tender.

4 Stir water into cornstarch in small bowl until smooth. Add to stew; cook and stir over medium heat 3 minutes or until thickened. Garnish with parsley.

MAKES 6 SERVINGS

CLASSIC PESTO WITH LINGUINE

12 ounces uncooked linguine

2 tablespoons butter

¼ cup plus 1 tablespoon
    olive oil, divided

2 tablespoons pine nuts

1 cup tightly packed
    fresh basil leaves

2 cloves garlic

¼ teaspoon salt

¼ cup grated Parmesan
    cheese

1½ tablespoons grated
    Romano cheese

1 Cook linguine according to package directions; drain. Toss with butter in large serving bowl; set aside and keep warm.

2 Meanwhile, heat 1 tablespoon oil in small skillet over medium-low heat. Add pine nuts; cook and stir 30 to 45 seconds or until lightly browned, shaking skillet constantly. Remove with slotted spoon; drain on paper towel-lined plate.

3 Combine toasted pine nuts, basil, garlic and salt in food processor or blender. With motor running, add remaining ¼ cup oil in slow, steady stream; process until well blended and pine nuts are finely chopped.

4 Transfer basil mixture to small bowl; stir in Parmesan and Romano.*

5 Add pesto sauce to pasta; toss until well coated. Serve immediately.

Pesto sauce can be stored at this point in an airtight container; pour thin layer of olive oil over pesto, cover and refrigerate up to 1 week. Bring to room temperature before using; proceed as directed in step 5.

**MAKES 4 SERVINGS
(ABOUT ¾ CUP PESTO SAUCE)**

FRENCH LENTIL SOUP

3 tablespoons olive oil

1 medium onion, chopped

1 carrot, chopped

1 stalk celery, chopped

1 clove garlic, minced

8 ounces dried lentils, rinsed and sorted

3 cups vegetable broth

1 can (about 14 ounces) stewed tomatoes

2 tablespoons balsamic vinegar, divided

Salt and black pepper

½ cup grated Parmesan cheese (optional)

1 Heat oil in large skillet over medium heat. Add onion, carrot, celery and garlic; cook 8 minutes or until vegetables are tender but not browned, stirring occasionally.

2 Stir in lentils, broth, tomatoes and 1½ tablespoons vinegar; bring to a boil over high heat. Reduce heat to low; cover and simmer 30 minutes or until lentils are tender.

3 Stir in remaining ½ tablespoon vinegar; season with salt and pepper. Sprinkle with cheese, if desired.

MAKES 4 TO 6 SERVINGS

BASQUE CHICKEN WITH PEPPERS

1 whole chicken (4 pounds), cut into 8 pieces

Salt and black pepper

1½ tablespoons olive oil

1 onion, chopped

2 cloves garlic, minced

3 bell peppers (red, yellow and green), cut into strips

8 ounces small brown mushrooms, halved

1 can (about 14 ounces) stewed tomatoes

½ cup chicken broth

½ cup dry red wine

3 ounces tomato paste

1 sprig fresh marjoram (optional)

1 teaspoon salt

1 teaspoon smoked paprika

½ teaspoon black pepper

4 ounces diced prosciutto

Hot cooked rice

Slow Cooker Directions

1 Season chicken with salt and black pepper.

2 Heat oil in large skillet over medium-high heat. Add chicken in batches; cook until well browned on all sides. Remove to slow cooker.

3 Add onion and garlic to skillet; cook and stir over medium-low heat 3 minutes or until softened. Add bell peppers and mushrooms to skillet; cook and stir 3 minutes. Add tomatoes, broth, wine, tomato paste, marjoram, if desired, 1 teaspoon salt, paprika and ½ teaspoon black pepper; cook 3 to 4 minutes. Pour over chicken in slow cooker.

4 Cover; cook on LOW 5 to 6 hours or on HIGH 4 hours or until chicken is cooked through.

5 Transfer chicken to serving platter. Spoon vegetables and sauce over chicken. Sprinkle with prosciutto; serve with rice.

MAKES 4 TO 6 SERVINGS

POLAND

POTATO PIEROGI

4 medium potatoes
(about 1½ pounds),
peeled and quartered

⅓ cup milk

2 tablespoons butter

2 tablespoons chopped
green onion, plus
additional for garnish

1 teaspoon salt, divided

½ teaspoon white pepper,
divided

2¾ cups all-purpose flour

1 cup sour cream

1 whole egg

1 egg yolk

1 tablespoon vegetable oil

Melted butter, cooked
crumbled bacon or
sour cream (optional)

1 For filling, place potatoes in medium saucepan; cover with water. Bring to a boil over high heat. Reduce heat to low; simmer, uncovered, 20 minutes or until tender. Drain and place in large bowl.

2 Mash potatoes. Stir in milk, butter, 2 tablespons green onion, ½ teaspoon salt and ¼ teaspoon pepper until blended (mixture will be stiff). Set aside to cool.

3 For dough, combine flour, sour cream, whole egg, egg yolk, oil, remaining ½ teaspoon salt and ¼ teaspoon pepper in medium bowl; mix well.

4 Turn out dough onto lightly floured surface. Knead 3 to 5 minutes or until soft and pliable but not sticky. Let dough rest, covered, 10 minutes. Divide dough in half. Roll out each half into 13-inch circle on lightly floured surface with lightly floured rolling pin. Cut out dough with 2½-inch-round cutter.

5 Place 1 rounded teaspoon potato filling in center of each dough circle. Moisten edges of circles with water and fold in half; press edges firmly to seal. Twist edges of dough, if desired.

6 Bring 4 quarts lightly salted water to a boil in large saucepan or Dutch oven over high heat. Cook pierogi in batches 10 minutes; remove to serving dish with slotted spoon. Drizzle with melted butter; top with bacon and additional green onions or serve with sour cream, if desired.

MAKES ABOUT 5 DOZEN PIEROGI

BEEF AND BEET BORSCHT

2 cans (15 ounces each) julienned beets

1 cup buttermilk

½ teaspoon salt

⅛ teaspoon black pepper

⅛ teaspoon ground cloves

1 cup beef broth

4 ounces thinly sliced deli roast beef, cut into short thin strips

¼ cup sour cream

Finely chopped fresh parsley

1 Drain beets, reserving 1 cup liquid. Place half of beets in food processor; process until finely chopped. Add buttermilk, salt, pepper and cloves; process until smooth. Transfer to medium bowl.

2 Stir in remaining beets, broth, reserved beet liquid and roast beef; mix well. Cover and refrigerate at least 2 hours or up to 24 hours.

3 Top with sour cream; sprinkle with parsley.

MAKES 4 SERVINGS

SPAGHETTI ALLA BOLOGNESE

2 tablespoons olive oil

1 pound ground beef

1 medium onion, chopped

½ small carrot, finely chopped

½ stalk celery, finely chopped

1 cup dry white wine

½ cup milk

⅛ teaspoon ground nutmeg

1 can (about 14 ounces) whole peeled tomatoes, coarsely chopped, juice reserved

1 cup beef broth

3 tablespoons tomato paste

1 teaspoon salt

1 teaspoon dried basil

½ teaspoon dried thyme

⅛ teaspoon black pepper

1 bay leaf

1 pound uncooked spaghetti

1 cup grated Parmesan cheese

1 Heat oil in large saucepan over medium heat. Add beef; cook 6 to 8 minutes, stirring to break up meat. Drain fat.

2 Add onion, carrot and celery; cook and stir 2 minutes. Stir in wine; cook 4 to 6 minutes or until wine has evaporated. Stir in milk and nutmeg; cook 3 to 4 minutes or until milk has almost evaporated. Remove from heat.

3 Press tomatoes with reserved juice through sieve into meat mixture; discard seeds.

4 Stir in broth, tomato paste, salt, basil, thyme, pepper and bay leaf; bring to a boil over medium-high heat. Reduce heat to low; simmer 1 to 1½ hours or until most liquid has evaporated and sauce thickens, stirring frequently. Remove and discard bay leaf.

5 Cook spaghetti according to package directions; drain. Combine spaghetti and meat sauce in large bowl; toss gently to coat. Sprinkle with cheese.

MAKES 4 TO 6 SERVINGS

HUNGARIAN BEEF GOULASH

¼ cup all-purpose flour

1 tablespoon Hungarian sweet paprika

1½ teaspoons salt

½ teaspoon Hungarian hot paprika

½ teaspoon black pepper

2 pounds beef stew meat

¼ cup vegetable oil, divided

1 large onion, chopped

4 cloves garlic, minced

2 cans (about 14 ounces each) beef broth

1 can (about 14 ounces) stewed tomatoes, undrained

1 cup water

1 tablespoon dried marjoram

1 green bell pepper, chopped

3 cups uncooked thin egg noodles

Sour cream

1 Combine flour, sweet paprika, salt, hot paprika and black pepper in large resealable food storage bag. Add half of beef. Seal bag; shake to coat well. Remove beef to large bowl. Repeat with remaining beef.

2 Heat 1½ tablespoons oil in Dutch oven over medium heat. Add half of beef; cook until browned on all sides. Remove to large bowl. Repeat with 1½ tablespoons oil and remaining beef; remove to bowl.

3 Heat remaining 1 tablespoon oil in Dutch oven. Add onion and garlic; cook 8 minutes or until tender, stirring frequently.

4 Return beef and any accumulated juices to Dutch oven. Add broth, tomatoes with juice, water and marjoram; bring to a boil over medium-high heat. Reduce heat to low; cover and simmer 1½ hours or until beef is tender, stirring once.

5 Stir in bell pepper and noodles; cover and cook about 8 minutes or until noodles are tender, stirring once. Top with sour cream.

MAKES 8 SERVINGS

IRELAND

LAMB AND MINT HAND PIES

2 cups plus 1 tablespoon all-purpose flour, divided

1 teaspoon salt, divided

10 tablespoons cold butter, cut into small pieces

7 to 8 tablespoons ice water

1 pound ground lamb

1 small onion, finely chopped

1 carrot, finely chopped

½ cup reduced-sodium beef broth

1 teaspoon Dijon mustard

¼ teaspoon black pepper

1 tablespoon chopped fresh mint

½ cup (2 ounces) shredded Irish Cheddar cheese

1 egg, lightly beaten

1 For dough, combine 2 cups flour and ½ teaspoon salt in medium bowl. Cut in butter with pastry blender or two knives until mixture resembles coarse crumbs. Add water, 1 tablespoon at a time, stirring with fork until loose dough forms. Knead dough in bowl 1 to 2 times until it comes together. Divide dough into four pieces; press each into 4-inch disc. Wrap dough with plastic wrap; freeze 15 minutes.

2 Meanwhile for filling, heat large skillet over medium-high heat. Add lamb; cook 7 to 8 minutes or until lightly browned, stirring occasionally. Drain; remove to plate. Add onion and carrot to skillet; cook 2 to 3 minutes or until vegetables begin to soften, stirring occasionally. Stir in lamb; cook 1 minute. Add remaining 1 tablespoon flour; cook and stir 1 minute. Add broth, mustard, remaining ½ teaspoon salt and pepper; cook over medium heat 2 minutes or until thickened. Remove from heat; stir in mint. Cool 10 minutes. Stir in cheese.

3 Preheat oven to 400°F. Line large baking sheet with parchment paper or spray with nonstick cooking spray.

4 Working with one disc at a time, roll out dough into 9-inch circle on lightly floured surface. Cut out four circles with 4-inch round cookie cutter (16 circles total). Place eight circles on prepared baking sheet. Top each with one eighth of lamb filling, leaving ½-inch border around edge of circle. Top with remaining dough circles, pressing edges to seal. Press edges again with tines of fork. Brush tops with egg; cut 1-inch slit in top of each pie with tip of knife.

5 Bake 28 to 30 minutes or until golden brown. Serve hot or at room temperature.

MAKES 4 MAIN-DISH OR 8 APPETIZER SERVINGS

GREECE

MEDITERRANEAN CHICKEN KABOBS

2 pounds boneless skinless chicken breasts or chicken tenders, cut into 1-inch pieces

1 small eggplant, peeled and cut into 1-inch pieces

1 medium zucchini, cut crosswise into ½-inch slices

2 medium onions, cut into wedges

16 medium mushrooms, stemmed

16 cherry tomatoes

1 cup chicken broth

⅔ cup balsamic vinegar

3 tablespoons olive oil

2 tablespoons dried mint

4 teaspoons dried basil

1 tablespoon dried oregano

Salt and black pepper

Hot cooked couscous

1 Alternately thread chicken, eggplant, zucchini, onions, mushrooms and tomatoes onto 8 large metal skewers or 16 medium metal or bamboo skewers; place in large glass baking dish.

2 Combine broth, vinegar, oil, mint, basil and oregano in small bowl; pour over kabobs. Sprinkle generously with salt and pepper. Cover and marinate in refrigerator 2 hours, turning occasionally. Remove kabobs from marinade; discard marinade.

3 Preheat broiler. Broil kabobs 6 inches from heat 10 to 15 minutes or until chicken is cooked through (165°F), turning kabobs halfway through cooking time. Serve with couscous.

MAKES 8 SERVINGS

 SPAIN

EMPANADILLAS

1 tablespoon olive oil

1 clove garlic, minced

1 shallot, thinly sliced

6 cups baby spinach (about 6 ounces)

¾ cup shredded manchego cheese or Swiss cheese

¼ cup pine nuts

¼ teaspoon salt

¼ teaspoon red pepper flakes

⅛ teaspoon black pepper

1 package (10 ounces) frozen puff pastry shells, thawed

All-purpose flour

1 Preheat oven to 400°F. Line baking sheet with parchment paper.

2 Heat oil in large nonstick skillet over medium-high heat. Add garlic and shallot; cook and stir 30 seconds. Add spinach; cook and stir 3 minutes or until spinach is wilted. Remove from heat; stir in cheese, pine nuts, salt, red pepper flakes and black pepper. Set aside to cool completely.

3 Roll out pastry shells into 5-inch circles on lightly floured surface. Place 3 tablespoons spinach mixture on one half of each circle. Brush edges of pastry with water. Fold pastry in half over filling; press edges with fork dipped in flour to seal. Place on prepared baking sheet.

4 Bake 20 minutes or until pastry is puffed and golden brown. Remove to wire rack. Serve warm.

MAKES 6 SERVINGS

RASPBERRY CLAFOUTIS

3 eggs

⅓ cup sugar

1 cup half-and-half

2 tablespoons butter, melted and slightly cooled

½ teaspoon vanilla

⅔ cup almond flour

Pinch salt

2 containers (6 ounces each) fresh raspberries

1 Preheat oven to 325°F. Generously grease 9-inch ceramic pie plate or tart pan.

2 Beat eggs and sugar in large bowl with electric mixer at medium speed 4 minutes or until pale and slightly thickened. Add half-and-half, butter and vanilla; whisk to combine. Gradually whisk in almond flour and salt. Pour enough batter into prepared pie plate to just cover bottom. Bake 10 minutes or until set.

3 Remove pie plate from oven. Scatter raspberries evenly over baked batter. Stir remaining batter; pour over raspberries.

4 Bake 40 to 45 minutes or until center is set and top is golden. Cool completely on wire rack. Refrigerate leftovers.

MAKES 8 TO 10 SERVINGS

KIELBASA, CABBAGE AND ONIONS

2 tablespoons olive oil

1 pound kielbasa, cut in half lengthwise then cut diagonally into ¾-inch slices

1 onion, thinly sliced

2 teaspoons fennel seeds

1 teaspoon caraway seeds

1 clove garlic, minced

½ cup water

1 pound cabbage (6 cups or ½ head), thinly sliced

2 pounds (5 medium) unpeeled red potatoes, cut into ¾-inch pieces

1 bottle (12 ounces) lager beer or ale

½ teaspoon salt

¼ teaspoon black pepper

1 Heat oil in large skillet over medium heat. Add kielbasa; cook 5 minutes or until browned, stirring occasionally. Remove to plate with slotted spoon.

2 Add onion, fennel seeds, caraway seeds and garlic to skillet; cook and stir 3 minutes or until onion is softened. Stir in water, scraping up browned bits from bottom of skillet. Add cabbage and potatoes; cook 10 minutes or until cabbage is wilted, stirring occasionally.

3 Stir in lager; cover and cook over medium-low heat 15 minutes or until potatoes are tender. Season with salt and pepper; cook over medium heat 15 minutes or until liquid has reduced to sauce consistency. Return kielbasa to skillet; cook until heated through.

MAKES 6 SERVINGS

FRANCE

FRENCH CARROT QUICHE

1 tablespoon butter

1 pound carrots, cut crosswise into ¼-inch slices

¼ cup chopped green onions

½ teaspoon herbes de Provence

1 cup milk

¼ cup whipping cream

½ cup all-purpose flour

2 eggs, lightly beaten

½ teaspoon minced fresh thyme

¼ teaspoon ground nutmeg

¼ teaspoon salt

½ cup (2 ounces) shredded Gruyère or Swiss cheese

1 Preheat oven to 350°F. Grease four shallow 1-cup baking dishes or 9-inch quiche dish or shallow casserole.

2 Melt butter in large skillet over medium heat. Add carrots, green onions and herbes de Provence; cook and stir 5 to 7 minutes or until carrots are tender.

3 Meanwhile, combine milk and cream in medium bowl; gradually whisk in flour. Stir in eggs, thyme, nutmeg and salt until well blended.

4 Spread carrot mixture in prepared dishes; top with milk mixture. Sprinkle with cheese.

5 Bake 20 to 25 minutes for individual quiches or 30 to 40 minutes for 9-inch quiche or until firm. Serve warm or at room temperature.

MAKES 4 SERVINGS

SWEDEN

SWEDISH LIMPA BREAD

1¾ to 2 cups all-purpose flour, divided

½ cup rye flour

1 package (¼ ounce) active dry yeast

1 tablespoon sugar

1½ teaspoons grated orange peel

1 teaspoon salt

½ teaspoon whole fennel seeds, crushed

½ teaspoon whole caraway seeds, crushed

¾ cup plus 4 teaspoons water, divided

4 tablespoons molasses, divided

2 tablespoons butter

1 teaspoon instant coffee granules

¼ teaspoon whole fennel seeds

¼ teaspoon whole caraway seeds

1 Combine 1½ cups all-purpose flour, rye flour, yeast, sugar, orange peel, salt and crushed seeds in large bowl. Heat ¾ cup water, 3 tablespoons molasses and butter in small saucepan over low heat to 120° to 130°F. Stir in coffee. Stir into flour mixture with rubber spatula to form soft but sticky dough. Gradually add additional all-purpose flour to form rough dough.

2 Turn out dough onto lightly floured surface. Knead 2 minutes or until soft dough forms, gradually adding remaining all-purpose flour to prevent sticking, if necessary. Cover with inverted bowl; let rest 5 minutes. Knead 5 to 8 minutes or until smooth and elastic. Shape dough into a ball. Place in large greased bowl; turn to grease top. Cover and let rise in warm place 1 hour and 15 minutes or until almost doubled in size.

3 Punch down dough. Grease 8½×4½-inch loaf pan. Roll dough into 12×7-inch rectangle. Starting with one short end, roll up tightly. Pinch seams and ends to seal. Place seam-side down in prepared pan. Cover loosely and let rise in warm place 1 hour or until doubled in size.

4 Preheat oven to 350°F. Stir remaining 1 tablespoon molasses and 4 teaspoons water in small bowl; set aside. Make three diagonal slashes in top of dough with sharp knife.

5 Bake 40 to 45 minutes or until loaf sounds hollow when tapped, brushing with molasses mixture and sprinkling with whole fennel and caraway seeds halfway through baking time. Brush again with molasses mixture during last 10 minutes of baking. Cool in pan on wire rack 5 minutes. Remove to wire rack; cool completely.

MAKES 1 LOAF

ENGLISH-STYLE SCONES

3 eggs, divided

½ cup whipping cream

1½ teaspoons vanilla

2 cups all-purpose flour

2 teaspoons baking powder

¼ teaspoon salt

¼ cup (½ stick) cold butter, cut into small pieces

¼ cup finely chopped pitted dates

¼ cup golden raisins or currants

1 teaspoon water

6 tablespoons orange marmalade

6 tablespoons softly whipped cream or crème fraîche

1 Preheat oven to 375°F. Line large baking sheet with parchment paper.

2 Whisk 2 eggs, cream and vanilla in medium bowl until blended. Combine flour, baking powder and salt in medium bowl. Cut in butter with pastry blender or two knives until mixture resembles coarse crumbs. Stir in dates and raisins. Add cream mixture; stir just until dry ingredients are moistened.

3 Turn out dough onto lightly floured surface; knead four times with floured hands. Place dough on prepared baking sheet; pat into 8-inch circle. Gently score dough into six wedges with sharp wet knife, cutting three fourths of the way through dough. Beat remaining egg and water in small bowl; brush lightly over dough.

4 Bake 18 to 20 minutes or until golden brown. Remove to wire rack to cool 5 minutes. Cut into wedges; serve warm with marmalade and whipped cream.

MAKES 6 SCONES

FRANCE

GANNAT (FRENCH CHEESE BREAD)

1 package (¼ ounce)
    active dry yeast

1 teaspoon sugar

4 to 6 tablespoons warm
    water (105° to 115°F)

2½ cups all-purpose flour

¼ cup (½ stick) butter,
    softened

1 teaspoon salt

2 eggs

1 cup (4 ounces) shredded
    Emmentaler Swiss,
    Gruyère, sharp Cheddar
    or Swiss cheese

1 teaspoon vegetable oil

1 Dissolve yeast and sugar in 4 tablespoons warm water in small bowl; let stand 5 minutes or until bubbly.

2 Combine flour, butter and salt in food processor; process 15 seconds or until blended. Add yeast mixture and eggs; process 15 seconds or just until blended.

3 With motor running, slowly drizzle just enough water through feed tube so dough forms a ball that cleans side of bowl. Process until ball turns around bowl about 25 times. Let dough rest 1 to 2 minutes. With motor running, drizzle in enough remaining water to make dough soft, smooth and satiny. Process until dough turns around bowl about 15 times.

4 Turn out dough onto lightly floured surface; shape into a ball. Place dough in greased bowl; turn to grease top. Cover and let rise in warm place about 1 hour or until doubled in size.

5 Spray 9-inch round cake pan or pie plate with nonstick cooking spray. Punch down dough. Place dough on lightly greased surface; knead cheese into dough. Roll or pat into 8-inch circle; brush with oil. Let rise in warm place about 45 minutes or until doubled in size. Preheat oven to 375°F.

6 Bake 30 to 35 minutes or until browned and bread sounds hollow when tapped. Remove to wire rack to cool completely.

MAKES 1 LOAF

SPANISH CHURROS

Churros

- 1 cup water
- ¼ cup (½ stick) butter
- 6 tablespoons granulated sugar, divided
- ¼ teaspoon salt
- 1 cup all-purpose flour
- 2 eggs
  Vegetable oil for frying
- 1 teaspoon ground cinnamon

Hot Fudge Sauce

- 2 cups whipping cream
- ½ cup light corn syrup
- ¾ cup packed dark brown sugar
- ⅓ cup cocoa powder
- 1 teaspoon kosher salt
- 8 ounces bittersweet chocolate, chopped
- ¼ cup (½ stick) cold butter

1 Combine water, ¼ cup butter, 2 tablespoons granulated sugar and salt in medium saucepan; bring to a boil over high heat. Remove from heat; add flour. Beat with spoon until dough forms a ball and releases from side of pan. Vigorously beat in eggs, one at a time, until mixture is smooth. Spoon dough into pastry bag fitted with large star tip. Pipe 3×1-inch strips onto waxed paper-lined baking sheet. Freeze 20 minutes.

2 Meanwhile, for hot fudge sauce, combine cream, corn syrup and brown sugar in large saucepan; bring to a boil over medium-high heat. Cook 2 minutes, stirring occasionally. Reduce heat to low; whisk in cocoa, 1 teaspoon salt and chocolate. Whisk 1 minute or until chocolate is melted and mixture is smooth. Turn off heat; whisk in ¼ cup cold butter. Pour into serving bowl; cool to room temperature.

3 Heat ¾ inch oil in large skillet to 375°F; adjust heat to maintain temperature. Transfer frozen dough, 4 to 5 churros at a time, to hot oil with large spatula. Fry 3 to 4 minutes or until deep golden brown, turning once. Remove to paper towel-lined baking sheet with slotted spoon to drain.

4 Combine remaining 4 tablespoons granulated sugar and cinnamon in paper bag. Add warm churros, one at a time; close bag and shake to coat. Remove to wire rack; cool completely. Store tightly covered at room temperature or freeze up to 3 months.

MAKES ABOUT 3 DOZEN CHURROS

CHOCOLATE MACARONS

1 cup powdered sugar

⅔ cup blanched almond flour

3 tablespoons unsweetened cocoa powder

3 egg whites, at room temperature*

¼ cup granulated sugar

Chocolate Ganache (page 97), chocolate-hazelnut spread or raspberry jam

For best results, separate the eggs while cold. Leave the egg whites at room temperature for 3 or 4 hours. Reserve yolks in refrigerator for another use.

1 Line two cookie sheets with parchment paper. Double cookie sheets by placing another sheet underneath each to protect macarons from burning or cracking. *Do not use insulated cookie sheets.*

2 Combine powdered sugar, almond flour and cocoa in food processor. Pulse 2 to 3 minutes or until well combined into very fine powder, scraping bowl occasionally. Sift mixture twice. Discard any remaining large pieces.

3 Beat egg whites in large bowl with electric mixer at high speed until foamy. Gradually add granulated sugar, beating at high speed 2 to 3 minutes or until mixture forms stiff, shiny peaks, scraping bowl occasionally.

4 Add half of flour mixture to egg whites. Stir with spatula to combine (about 12 strokes). Repeat with remaining flour mixture. Mix about 15 strokes more by pressing against side of bowl and scooping from bottom until batter is smooth and shiny. Check consistency by dropping spoonful of batter onto plate. It should have a peak which quickly relaxes back into batter. *Do not overmix or undermix.*

5 Attach ½-inch plain piping tip to pastry bag. Scoop batter into bag. Pipe 1-inch circles about 2 inches apart onto prepared cookie sheets. Rap cookie sheet on flat surface to remove air bubbles and set aside. Repeat with remaining batter. Let macarons rest, uncovered, until tops harden slightly; this takes from 15 minutes on dry days to 1 hour in more humid conditions. Gently touch top of macaron to check. When batter does not stick, macarons are ready to bake.

6 Meanwhile, preheat oven to 375°F. Position rack in center of oven. Place one sheet of macarons in oven. *After 5 minutes, reduce heat to 325°F.* Bake 10 to 13 minutes, checking at 5-minute intervals. If macarons begin to brown, cover loosely with foil and reduce oven temperature or prop oven door open slightly with wooden spoon. Repeat with remaining cookie sheet.

7 Cool completely on cookie sheet on wire rack. While cooling, if cookies appear to be sticking to parchment, lift parchment edges and spray pan underneath lightly with water. Steam will help release macarons. Prepare Chocolate Ganache.

8 Match same size cookies; spread bottom macaron with ganache and top with another. Store macarons in covered container in refrigerator 4 to 5 days. Freeze for longer storage.

MAKES 16 TO 20 MACARONS

Chocolate Ganache

Place 4 ounces chopped semisweet or bittersweet chocolate in shallow bowl. Heat ½ cup whipping cream in small saucepan until bubbles form around edges. Pour cream over chocolate; let stand 5 minutes. Stir until smooth.

HUNGARIAN LEMON POPPY SEED COOKIES

Cookies

- ⅔ cup granulated sugar
- ½ cup (1 stick) butter, softened
- 1 egg
- 2 teaspoons grated lemon peel
- 1¼ cups all-purpose flour
- ½ teaspoon baking soda
- ¼ teaspoon salt
- 1 tablespoon poppy seeds

Glaze

- 1 cup powdered sugar
- 2 tablespoons lemon juice

1 Preheat oven to 350°F.

2 For cookies, beat granulated sugar and butter in large bowl with electric mixer at medium speed until creamy. Beat in egg and lemon peel.

3 Combine flour, baking soda and salt in small bowl; gradually add to butter mixture. Beat in poppy seeds at low speed. Drop dough by heaping teaspoonfuls 2 inches apart onto ungreased cookie sheets.

4 Bake 11 to 12 minutes or until edges are lightly browned. Cool on cookie sheets 1 minute. Remove to wire racks; cool completely.

5 For glaze, combine powdered sugar and lemon juice in small bowl; mix well. Drizzle glaze over cookies; let stand about 20 minutes or until glaze is set.

MAKES ABOUT 2 DOZEN COOKIES

MOZAMBIQUE

PERI–PERI CHICKEN

1 small red onion, coarsely chopped

1 roasted red pepper (about 3 ounces)

¼ cup olive oil

¼ cup lemon juice

2 tablespoons white vinegar

4 cloves garlic, minced

1 tablespoon smoked paprika

1½ teaspoons salt

1½ teaspoons red pepper flakes

1 teaspoon dried oregano

½ teaspoon black pepper

1 cut-up whole chicken (3 to 4 pounds)

1 Combine onion, roasted pepper, oil, lemon juice, vinegar, garlic, smoked paprika, salt, red pepper flakes, oregano and black pepper in blender or food processor; blend until smooth. Remove half of marinade to small bowl; cover and refrigerate until ready to use.

2 Use sharp knife to make several slashes in each piece of chicken (about ¼ inch deep). Place chicken in large resealable food storage bag. Pour remaining marinade over chicken; seal bag and turn to coat, massaging marinade into chicken. Marinate chicken in refrigerator at least 4 hours or overnight, turning occasionally.

3 Remove chicken from refrigerator about 30 minutes before cooking. Preheat oven to 400°F. Line baking sheet with foil. Arrange chicken on baking sheet.

4 Bake about 45 minutes or until chicken is cooked through (165°F), brushing with some of reserved marinade every 15 minutes. Serve with remaining marinade, if desired.

MAKES 4 SERVINGS

GHANA

WEST AFRICAN PEANUT SOUP

2 tablespoons vegetable oil

1 large onion, chopped

½ cup chopped roasted peanuts

1½ tablespoons minced fresh ginger

4 cloves garlic, minced (about 1 tablespoon)

1 teaspoon salt

4 cups vegetable broth

1 can (28 ounces) whole tomatoes, drained and coarsely chopped

2 sweet potatoes, peeled and cut into ½-inch pieces

¼ teaspoon ground red pepper

1 bunch Swiss chard or kale, stemmed and shredded

⅓ cup unsweetened peanut butter (creamy or chunky)

1 Heat oil in large saucepan over medium-high heat. Add onion; cook and stir 5 minutes or until softened. Add peanuts, ginger, garlic and salt; cook and stir 1 minute. Stir in broth, tomatoes, sweet potatoes and red pepper; bring to a boil. Reduce heat to medium; simmer 10 minutes.

2 Stir in chard and peanut butter; cook over medium-low heat 10 minutes or until vegetables are tender and soup is creamy.

MAKES 6 TO 8 SERVINGS

MOROCCO

SPICY–SWEET LAMB TAGINE WITH SAFFRON COUSCOUS

1 tablespoon olive oil

2 pounds boneless lamb shoulder or leg, cut into 1½- to 2-inch pieces

3 medium onions, cut into eighths

3 cloves garlic, minced

2 teaspoons ground ginger

2 teaspoons ground cinnamon

1 teaspoon black pepper

2 cups water

1 can (about 14 ounces) diced tomatoes

1 can (about 15 ounces) chickpeas, rinsed and drained

1 cup chopped pitted prunes

½ teaspoon salt

1 small butternut squash, peeled and cut into 1-inch pieces

1 medium zucchini, halved and sliced crosswise into 1-inch pieces

Saffron Couscous (page 105)

¼ cup chopped fresh cilantro or parsley

1 Heat oil in Dutch oven over high heat. Add lamb in two batches; cook until browned on all sides. Return all lamb to Dutch oven.

2 Add onions, garlic, ginger, cinnamon and pepper; stir 30 seconds or until spices are fragrant. Stir in 2 cups water and tomatoes; bring to a boil, scraping up browned bits from bottom of pan. Reduce heat to medium-low; cover and simmer 1 hour.

3 Remove 1 cup broth from lamb mixture; place in large saucepan and set aside.

4 Simmer lamb, covered, 30 minutes; add additional water, if necessary. Add chickpeas, prunes and salt; simmer 20 minutes or until lamb is tender. Uncover; simmer until broth is slightly thickened.

5 Add squash to broth in saucepan; cover and bring to a boil over high heat. Reduce heat to medium-low; simmer 20 minutes or until squash is tender. Add zucchini; simmer 10 to 15 minutes or until zucchini is tender. Remove from heat; cover to keep warm.

6 Prepare Saffron Couscous; place on large serving platter. Form well in center of couscous. Spoon lamb stew in center; top with vegetables. Sprinkle with cilantro.

MAKES 6 SERVINGS

SAFFRON COUSCOUS

2¼ cups water

1 tablespoon butter

¼ teaspoon salt

¼ teaspoon crushed saffron threads *or* pinch of powdered saffron

1½ cups uncooked couscous

1 Combine water, butter, salt and saffron in medium saucepan. Bring to a boil over high heat. Stir in couscous. Cover; remove from heat.

2 Let stand 5 minutes or until liquid is absorbed. Fluff couscous with fork.

MAKES 6 SERVINGS

JOLLOF RICE WITH EGGPLANT

1 medium eggplant (about 1¼ pounds), cut into 1-inch cubes

2 teaspoons salt, divided

4 tablespoons vegetable oil, divided

1 onion, chopped

1 green bell pepper, chopped

3 carrots, cut into ½-inch slices

2 cloves garlic, minced

1½ cups uncooked long grain rice

3 tablespoons tomato paste

1 tablespoon plus ½ teaspoon chili powder

1 teaspoon dried thyme

½ teaspoon ground ginger

1 can (28 ounces) diced tomatoes

3 cups vegetable broth

1 Place eggplant in colander. Toss with 1 teaspoon salt; let stand in sink 1 hour to drain. Rinse under cold water; drain and pat dry with paper towels.

2 Heat 1 tablespoon oil in large skillet over medium-high heat. Add half of eggplant; cook until browned on all sides, stirring occasionally. Remove to plate. Repeat with 1 tablespoon oil and remaining eggplant.

3 Heat remaining 2 tablespoons oil in large saucepan over medium heat. Add onion, bell pepper, carrots and garlic; cook and stir 5 minutes or until onion is translucent. Stir in rice, tomato paste, chili powder, thyme, ginger and remaining 1 teaspoon salt.

4 Stir in tomatoes and broth; bring to a boil. Reduce heat to low; cover and simmer 20 minutes.

5 Stir in eggplant; cover and simmer 10 minutes or until rice is tender, stirring in water by tablespoonfuls if rice seems dry.

MAKES 6 SERVINGS

Note

Jollof Rice (also spelled "jolof" or sometimes "djolof") is an important dish in many West African cultures, including Nigeria and Ghana.

MOROCCAN PORK AND POTATO CASSEROLE

2 tablespoons vegetable oil

1 pound pork stew meat, cut into 1-inch pieces

½ cup chopped onion

3 tablespoons all-purpose flour

1 can (about 14 ounces) diced tomatoes

¼ cup water

1 teaspoon ground ginger

1 teaspoon ground cumin

1 teaspoon ground cinnamon

½ teaspoon sugar

½ teaspoon salt

½ teaspoon black pepper

2 medium unpeeled red potatoes, cut into ½-inch pieces

1 large sweet potato, peeled and cut into ½-inch pieces

1 cup frozen lima beans, thawed and drained

1 cup frozen cut green beans, thawed and drained

¾ cup sliced carrots

1 Preheat oven to 325°F.

2 Heat oil in large skillet over medium-high heat. Add pork and onion; cook until pork is browned on all sides. Sprinkle with flour; stir until flour has absorbed pan juices. Cook 2 minutes.

3 Stir in tomatoes, water, ginger, cumin, cinnamon, sugar, salt and pepper; mix well. Transfer mixture to 2-quart casserole.

4 Bake 30 minutes. Stir in red potatoes, sweet potato, lima beans, green beans and carrots; cover and bake 1 hour or until potatoes are tender. Serve with pita bread.

MAKES 6 SERVINGS

TUNISIAN FISH WITH COUSCOUS

¼ cup olive oil

2 cups chopped onions

8 cloves garlic, minced

2 tablespoons tomato paste

1 tablespoon ground cumin

1 tablespoon paprika

½ teaspoon ground cinnamon

8 cups chicken or vegetable broth, divided

1½ pounds small potatoes, quartered

1 can (about 15 ounces) chickpeas, rinsed and drained

5 carrots, cut into 2×¼-inch strips

1 red bell pepper, cut into ½-inch strips

½ teaspoon salt

6 grouper fillets (about 5 ounces each)

2 cups uncooked couscous

1 Heat oil in large saucepan over medium heat. Add onions and garlic; cook and stir 5 minutes or until onions are tender. Add tomato paste, cumin, paprika and cinnamon; cook 1 minute, stirring constantly.

2 Add 5 cups broth; bring to a boil over high heat. Reduce heat to low; cover and simmer 10 minutes. Add potatoes; cover and simmer 10 minutes. Add chickpeas, carrots, bell pepper and salt; cover and simmer 5 minutes.

3 Rinse fish; pat dry with paper towels. Cut into 2×1-inch strips. Add fish to broth; cover and simmer 5 to 7 minutes or until fish begins to flake when tested with fork.

4 Bring remaining 3 cups broth to a boil in medium saucepan over medium-high heat. Stir in couscous. Remove from heat; cover and let stand 5 minutes or until liquid is absorbed. Fluff with fork.

5 Spoon couscous into shallow bowls; top with fish and vegetables.

MAKES 6 SERVINGS

MOROCCO

MOROCCAN CHICKEN MEATBALLS WITH APRICOTS AND ALMONDS

1 pound ground chicken, turkey or lamb

¾ teaspoon salt, divided

¼ teaspoon ground cinnamon

¼ teaspoon black pepper

1 tablespoon olive oil

1 small onion, chopped

1 cup sliced dried apricots

1 can (28 ounces) diced tomatoes

½ teaspoon red pepper flakes

½ teaspoon ground ginger

1 can (10½ ounces) condensed chicken broth

½ cup water

1 cup pearl couscous*

¼ cup sliced almonds, toasted

Pearl couscous, also called Israeli couscous, is available in large supermarkets with other grains and pastas.

1 Preheat oven to 325°F. Spray 11×7-inch baking dish with nonstick cooking spray.

2 Combine chicken, ½ teaspoon salt, cinnamon and black pepper in medium bowl. Shape into 1-inch balls. Heat oil in large skillet over medium heat. Add meatballs; cook until browned on all sides. Remove to plate.

3 Add onion and apricots to skillet; cook 5 minutes or until onion is tender. Stir in tomatoes, remaining ¼ teaspoon salt, red pepper flakes and ginger; cook 5 minutes.

4 Meanwhile, bring broth and water to a boil in small saucepan over high heat. Stir in couscous. Reduce heat to low; cover and simmer 10 minutes or until couscous is tender and almost all liquid has been absorbed. Drain, if necessary.

5 Spoon couscous into prepared baking dish. Top with meatballs and tomato mixture.

6 Bake 20 minutes or until chicken is cooked through. Sprinkle with almonds.

MAKES 4 TO 6 SERVINGS

EAST AFRICAN MUSHROOM PILAU

5 whole cardamom pods

1 teaspoon cumin seeds

5 whole cloves

1 tablespoon butter

1 tablespoon vegetable oil

1 onion, finely chopped

8 ounces white or cremini mushrooms, cut into ¼-inch slices

1 cup uncooked basmati rice, rinsed well in fine-mesh strainer

1 bay leaf

1 teaspoon salt

½ teaspoon ground turmeric

1 cinnamon stick

1 can (about 14 ounces) vegetable broth

¼ cup water

¼ cup cashews

1 Preheat oven to 250°F. Remove seeds from cardamom pods; discard pods. Combine cardamom seeds, cumin and cloves in baking pan.

2 Bake 20 to 30 minutes or until spices are fragrant, stirring every 10 minutes. Transfer warm spices to clean coffee or spice grinder; grind to fine powder (or use mortar and pestle to pulverize). Set aside.

3 Heat butter and oil in large skillet over medium heat. Add onion; cook and stir 5 minutes or until softened. Add mushrooms; cook and stir 5 minutes.

4 Stir in rice, bay leaf, salt, turmeric, cinnamon stick and ground roasted spices; cook and stir 2 minutes or until spices are fragrant.

5 Stir in broth and water; bring to a boil. Reduce heat to low; cover and simmer 15 minutes or until rice is tender and liquid is absorbed.

6 Remove and discard bay leaf and cinnamon stick; fluff rice with fork. Let stand, covered, 5 minutes. Sprinkle with cashews.

MAKES 4 TO 6 SERVINGS

 *Africa*

 MOROCCO

SPICED CHICKPEAS AND COUSCOUS

1 can (about 14 ounces) vegetable broth

1 teaspoon ground coriander

½ teaspoon ground cardamom

½ teaspoon ground turmeric

½ teaspoon hot pepper sauce

¼ teaspoon salt

⅛ teaspoon ground cinnamon

1 cup shredded or julienned carrots

1 can (about 15 ounces) chickpeas, rinsed and drained

1 cup frozen peas

1 cup uncooked couscous

2 tablespoons chopped fresh mint or parsley

1 Combine broth, coriander, cardamom, turmeric, hot pepper sauce, salt and cinnamon in large saucepan; bring to a boil over high heat. Add carrots; reduce heat to low and simmer 5 minutes.

2 Add chickpeas and green peas; return to a simmer. Simmer, uncovered, 2 minutes.

3 Stir in couscous. Remove from heat; cover and let stand 5 minutes or until liquid is absorbed. Sprinkle with mint.

MAKES 6 SERVINGS

CHINA

SPICY CHINESE PEPPER STEAK

1 boneless beef top sirloin steak (about 1 pound) or tenderloin tips, cut into thin strips

1 tablespoon cornstarch

3 cloves garlic, minced

½ teaspoon red pepper flakes

2 tablespoons peanut or canola oil, divided

1 green bell pepper, cut into thin strips

1 red bell pepper, cut into thin strips

¼ cup oyster sauce

2 tablespoons soy sauce

3 tablespoons chopped fresh cilantro or green onions

1 Combine beef, cornstarch, garlic and red pepper flakes in medium bowl; toss to coat.

2 Heat 1 tablespoon oil in wok or large skillet over medium-high heat. Add bell peppers; stir-fry 3 minutes. Remove to small bowl. Add remaining 1 tablespoon oil and beef mixture to wok; stir-fry 4 to 5 minutes or until beef is barely pink in center.

3 Add oyster sauce and soy sauce to wok; cook and stir 1 minute. Return bell peppers to wok; cook and stir 1 to 2 minutes or until sauce thickens. Sprinkle with cilantro.

MAKES 4 SERVINGS

JAPAN

CHICKEN GYOZA

Dipping Sauce
(recipe follows)

4 ounces ground chicken

¼ cup finely chopped
napa cabbage

1 green onion, minced

1½ teaspoons soy sauce

½ teaspoon minced fresh
ginger

½ teaspoon cornstarch

22 gyoza or wonton wrappers
(about half of 10-ounce
package)

2 tablespoons vegetable oil

1 Prepare Dipping Sauce; set aside.

2 Combine chicken, cabbage, green onion, soy
sauce and ginger in medium bowl; mix well.
Stir in cornstarch until well blended.

3 Place 1 rounded teaspoonful chicken mixture
in center of gyoza wrapper. Moisten edges of
wrapper with wet finger. Pull sides of wrapper
together; press to seal semicircle. Pleat edges
of gyoza by making small folds. Place on lightly
oiled surface while filling remaining gyoza.

4 Heat vegetable oil in large skillet over medium
heat. Add 8 to 10 gyoza to skillet; do not crowd.
Cook 3 minutes per side or until golden brown
and filling is cooked through. Keep warm while
cooking remaining gyoza. Serve with Dipping
Sauce.

**MAKES 22 GYOZA
(4 TO 6 APPETIZER SERVINGS)**

Dipping Sauce

Combine ¼ cup soy sauce, 2 teaspoons mirin
(Japanese sweet rice wine) and ¼ to ½ teaspoon
chili oil in small bowl; mix well.

THAILAND

SPICY THAI SHRIMP SOUP

1 tablespoon vegetable oil

1 pound medium raw
shrimp, peeled and
deveined, shells
reserved

1 jalapeño pepper, cut
into slivers

1 tablespoon paprika

¼ teaspoon ground red
pepper

4 cans (about 14 ounces
each) chicken broth

1 (½-inch) strip *each* lemon
and lime peel

1 can (15 ounces) straw
mushrooms, drained

Juice of 1 lemon

Juice of 1 lime

2 tablespoons soy sauce

1 red Thai pepper or red
jalapeño pepper *or*
¼ small red bell pepper,
cut into thin strips

¼ cup fresh cilantro leaves

1 Heat wok or large skillet over medium-high heat
1 minute. Add oil; heat 30 seconds. Add shrimp
and jalapeño pepper; stir-fry 1 minute. Add
paprika and ground red pepper; stir-fry 1 minute
or until shrimp are pink and opaque. Transfer to
medium bowl.

2 Add shrimp shells to wok; cook and stir
30 seconds. Add broth and lemon and lime
peels; bring to a boil. Reduce heat to low;
cover and simmer 15 minutes.

3 Remove and discard shells and peels with slotted
spoon. Add mushrooms and shrimp mixture to
broth; bring to a boil over medium heat. Stir
in lemon and lime juices, soy sauce and Thai
pepper; cook until heated through. Sprinkle
with cilantro. Serve immediately.

MAKES 4 SERVINGS

PRESSED SUSHI (OSHIZUSHI)

1½ cups Japanese short grain sushi rice

3 tablespoons seasoned rice vinegar

1 large red bell pepper

1 large yellow bell pepper

1 tablespoon tamari or soy sauce

1 tablespoon mirin (Japanese sweet rice wine)

¼ cup finely chopped unpeeled cucumber

4 ounces thinly sliced smoked salmon

Salmon roe (caviar) and pickled ginger (optional)

1 Prepare rice according to package directions; spread warm rice in large wooden bowl or on parchment paper-lined baking sheet. Sprinkle with vinegar; gently fold vinegar into rice with wooden spoon or spatula. Cover with damp clean cloth; set aside. *Do not refrigerate.*

2 Meanwhile, preheat broiler. Cut bell peppers lengthwise into quarters; place skin sides up on foil-lined baking sheet. Broil 3 to 4 inches from heat source 10 minutes or until skins are blackened. Wrap peppers in foil; let stand 10 minutes. Peel off and discard skins.

3 Line 8-inch square baking pan or glass dish with foil, allowing foil to extend over edges of pan for easy removal. Spoon half of rice into prepared pan; press down firmly. Arrange pepper pieces over rice in single layer, covering rice completely. Combine tamari and mirin in small cup; drizzle over peppers.

4 Combine remaining rice and cucumber in medium bowl. Spoon evenly over pepper layer; press down firmly. Arrange salmon over rice covering entire surface; press down firmly. Cover salmon with plastic wrap. Place another 8-inch square baking pan on top of plastic; weight down with two or three cans of food. Let stand at room temperature 1 hour or refrigerate up to 6 hours.

5 Remove weighted pan and plastic wrap. Use foil to transfer pressed sushi to cutting board; cut into squares or rectangles. Garnish with salmon roe and ginger.

MAKES 4 MAIN-DISH OR 8 SIDE-DISH SERVINGS

CUCUMBER SALAD

1 large cucumber (about 12 ounces)

2 tablespoons rice vinegar

2 tablespoons peanut or vegetable oil

2 tablespoons soy sauce

1½ teaspoons sugar

1 clove garlic, minced

¼ teaspoon red pepper flakes

1 Score cucumber lengthwise with tines of fork. Cut in half lengthwise; scrape out and discard seeds. Cut crosswise into ⅛-inch slices; place in medium bowl.

2 Combine vinegar, oil, soy sauce, sugar, garlic and red pepper flakes in small bowl; mix well. Pour dressing over cucumber; toss to coat. Cover and refrigerate at least 4 hours or up to 2 days.

MAKES 4 TO 6 SERVINGS

CHINA

BARBECUED PORK

¼ cup soy sauce

2 tablespoons dry red wine

1 green onion, sliced

1 tablespoon packed
brown sugar

1 tablespoon honey

2 teaspoons red food
coloring (optional)

1 clove garlic, minced

½ teaspoon ground
cinnamon

2 whole pork tenderloins
(about 12 ounces each),
trimmed

Hot cooked rice (optional)

1 Combine soy sauce, wine, green onion, brown sugar, honey, food coloring, if desired, garlic and cinnamon in large bowl; mix well. Add pork; turn to coat. Cover and refrigerate 1 hour or overnight, turning occasionally.

2 Preheat oven to 350°F. Line 13×9-inch baking pan with foil. Drain pork, reserving marinade. Place pork on wire rack in prepared pan.

3 Roast 30 to 45 minutes or until pork is 145°F, turning and basting frequently with reserved marinade during first 30 minutes of cooking. Discard any remaining marinade. Remove pork to cutting board; tent with foil and let rest 5 minutes. Cut into diagonal slices. Serve with rice, if desired.

**MAKES 4 MAIN-DISH
OR 8 APPETIZER SERVINGS**

DONBURI (BEEF AND RICE BOWL)

1 cup uncooked short or
    medium grain rice

3 teaspoons peanut or
    vegetable oil, divided

3 eggs, beaten

2 cups broccoli florets

1 small yellow onion,
    cut into thin wedges

1 pound boneless beef
    top sirloin steak,
    cut crosswise into
    thin strips

2 teaspoons cornstarch

¼ cup beef or chicken broth

3 tablespoons tamari
    or soy sauce

2 teaspoons dark sesame oil

¼ teaspoon red pepper
    flakes

¼ cup chopped fresh
    cilantro

¼ cup chopped green onions

1 Cook rice according to package directions.

2 Meanwhile, heat 1 teaspoon peanut oil in wok or medium skillet over medium heat. Add eggs; cook 2 minutes or until bottom of omelet is set. Turn omelet over and cook 1 minute. Slide onto cutting board; let cool. Roll up omelet and cut crosswise into thin slices.

3 Heat 1 teaspoon peanut oil in wok; add broccoli and onion. Cook 4 to 5 minutes, stirring occasionally. Transfer to medium bowl.

4 Combine beef and cornstarch in small bowl; toss to coat. Heat remaining 1 teaspoon peanut oil in wok. Add beef; stir-fry 2 minutes. Add broth, tamari, sesame oil and red pepper flakes; cook 2 minutes or until sauce thickens.

5 Stir in sliced omelet, vegetable mixture, cilantro and green onions; cook and stir 1 minute or until heated through. Serve over rice.

MAKES 4 SERVINGS

 CHINA

WONTON SOUP

4 ounces ground pork, chicken or turkey

¼ cup finely chopped water chestnuts

2 tablespoons soy sauce, divided

1 egg white, lightly beaten

1 teaspoon minced fresh ginger

12 wonton wrappers

6 cups chicken broth

1½ cups fresh spinach leaves, torn

1 cup thinly sliced cooked pork (optional)

½ cup diagonally sliced green onions

1 tablespoon dark sesame oil

Shredded carrot (optional)

1 Combine ground pork, water chestnuts, 1 tablespoon soy sauce, egg white and ginger in small bowl; mix well.

2 Arrange wonton wrappers on clean work surface. Spoon 1 teaspoon filling near bottom point. Fold bottom point of wrapper up over filling; fold side points over filling. Moisten inside edges with water; bring edges together firmly to seal. Repeat with remaining wrappers and filling. Keep finished wontons covered with plastic wrap while filling remaining wrappers to prevent drying out.

3 Combine broth and remaining 1 tablespoon soy sauce in large saucepan; bring to a boil over high heat. Reduce heat to medium; add wontons. Cook 4 minutes or until filling is cooked through.

4 Stir in spinach, sliced pork, if desired, and green onions; remove from heat. Stir in oil. Garnish with shredded carrot.

MAKES 4 SERVINGS

CHINA

BRAISED LION'S HEAD

Meatballs

- 1 pound ground pork
- 4 ounces raw shrimp, peeled and finely chopped
- ¼ cup sliced water chestnuts, finely chopped
- 1 egg, lightly beaten
- 1 green onion with top, finely chopped
- 1 tablespoon cornstarch
- 1 tablespoon dry sherry
- 1 tablespoon soy sauce
- 1 teaspoon minced fresh ginger
- ½ teaspoon salt
- ½ teaspoon sugar
- 2 tablespoons vegetable oil

Sauce

- 1½ cups chicken broth
- 2 tablespoons soy sauce
- ½ teaspoon sugar
- 1 head napa cabbage (1½ to 2 pounds), cut into large pieces
- 2 tablespoons cornstarch
- 3 tablespoons cold water
- 1 teaspoon dark sesame oil

1 For meatballs, combine all meatball ingredients except vegetable oil in large bowl; mix well. Shape mixture into eight balls.

2 Heat vegetable oil in wok or large nonstick skillet over medium-high heat. Add meatballs; cook 6 to 8 minutes until browned, stirring occasionally.

3 Transfer meatballs to large saucepan; discard drippings. Add broth, 2 tablespoons soy sauce and ½ teaspoon sugar; bring to a boil. Reduce heat to low; cover and simmer 30 minutes. Place cabbage over meatballs; cover and simmer 10 minutes.

4 Transfer cabbage and meatballs to serving platter with slotted spoon. Stir 2 tablespoons cornstarch into water in small bowl until smooth. Gradually add to saucepan, stirring constantly; cook until sauce is slightly thickened. Stir in sesame oil. Serve sauce over meatballs and cabbage.

MAKES 4 TO 6 SERVINGS

Asia

 VIETNAM

GRILLED VIETNAMESE–STYLE CHICKEN WINGS

3 pounds chicken wings
⅓ cup honey
¼ to ½ cup sliced lemongrass
¼ cup fish sauce
2 tablespoons chopped garlic
2 tablespoons chopped shallots
2 tablespoons chopped fresh ginger
2 tablespoons lime juice
2 tablespoons canola oil
Chopped fresh cilantro (optional)

1 Remove and discard wing tips. Cut each wing in half at joint. Place wings in large resealable food storage bag.

2 Combine honey, lemongrass, fish sauce, garlic, shallots, ginger, lime juice and oil in food processor; process until smooth. Pour over wings. Seal bag; turn to coat. Marinate in refrigerator 4 hours or overnight.

3 Prepare grill for direct cooking over medium heat or preheat grill pan. Preheat oven to 350°F.

4 Remove wings from marinade; reserve marinade. Grill wings 10 minutes or until browned, turning and basting occasionally with marinade. Discard any remaining marinade.

5 Arrange wings in single layer on baking sheet. Bake 20 minutes or until cooked through. Sprinkle with cilantro, if desired.

MAKES 6 TO 8 SERVINGS

MONGOLIAN BEEF

1¼ pounds beef flank steak

¼ cup cornstarch

3 tablespoons vegetable oil, divided

3 cloves garlic, minced

2 teaspoons grated fresh ginger

½ cup water

½ cup soy sauce

⅓ cup packed dark brown sugar

Pinch red pepper flakes

2 green onions, diagonally sliced into 1-inch pieces

Hot cooked rice (optional)

1 Cut flank steak in half lengthwise, then cut crosswise (against the grain) into ¼-inch slices. Combine beef and cornstarch in medium bowl; toss to coat.

2 Heat 1 tablespoon oil in wok or large skillet over high heat. Add half of beef in single layer (do not crowd); cook 1 to 2 minutes per side or until browned. Remove to clean bowl. Repeat with remaining beef and 1 tablespoon oil.

3 Heat remaining 1 tablespoon oil in wok over medium heat. Add garlic and ginger; cook and stir 30 seconds. Add water, soy sauce, brown sugar and red pepper flakes; bring to a boil, stirring until well blended. Cook 8 minutes or until slightly thickened, stirring occasionally.

4 Return beef to wok; cook 2 to 3 minutes or until sauce thickens and beef is heated through. Stir in green onions. Serve with rice, if desired.

MAKES 4 SERVINGS

 INDIA

PAKORAS

Tamarind Sauce
(recipe follows)
1½ cups chickpea flour
2 teaspoons salt
1 teaspoon baking soda
½ teaspoon ground turmeric
½ teaspoon chili powder
¼ teaspoon garlic powder
¾ cup water, divided
¼ cup plain yogurt
1 large zucchini, cut into
   ¼-inch slices
1 medium sweet potato,
   cut into ¼-inch slices
½ small butternut squash,
   peeled, seeded and cut
   into ¼-inch-thick slices
1 small Asian eggplant,
   cut into ¼-inch slices
4 cups canola oil

1 Prepare Tamarind Sauce; set aside.

2 Whisk flour, salt, baking soda, turmeric, chili powder and garlic powder in large bowl until well blended. Whisk ½ cup water and yogurt in small bowl until well blended. Add enough yogurt mixture to flour mixture to make thick batter (similar to pancake batter).

3 Combine vegetable slices and ¼ cup water in large microwavable bowl. Cover with plastic wrap; microwave on HIGH 2 minutes. Remove from microwave. Set aside to cool. Drain water; pat vegetables dry with paper towels.

4 Heat oil in deep saucepan to 350°F; adjust heat to maintain temperature.

5 Dip vegetable slices into batter; coat well. Working in batches, carefully place vegetables in hot oil. Fry about 30 seconds per side or until golden brown. Drain on paper towel-lined baking sheet.

MAKES 4 TO 6 SERVINGS

Tamarind Sauce

Combine 2 cups water, ⅓ cup sugar and 2 tablespoons tamarind paste in small saucepan; bring to a boil over high heat. Reduce heat to low; simmer until mixture is reduced by two thirds.

CHICKEN FRIED RICE

2 tablespoons vegetable oil, divided

12 ounces boneless skinless chicken breasts, cut into ½-inch cubes

   Salt and black pepper

2 tablespoons butter

2 cloves garlic, minced

½ sweet onion, diced

1 medium carrot, diced

2 green onions, thinly sliced

3 eggs

4 cups cooked rice*

3 tablespoons soy sauce

2 tablespoons sesame seeds

*For rice, cook 1½ cups rice according to package directions without oil or butter. Spread hot rice on large rimmed baking sheet; cool to room temperature. Refrigerate several hours or overnight. Measure 4 cups for recipe.

1 Heat 1 tablespoon oil in wok or large skillet over medium-high heat. Add chicken; season with salt and pepper. Cook and stir 5 to 6 minutes or until cooked through. Add butter and garlic; cook and stir 1 minute or until butter is melted. Remove to medium bowl.

2 Add sweet onion, carrot and green onions to wok; cook and stir over high heat 3 minutes or until vegetables are softened. Add to bowl with chicken.

3 Heat remaining 1 tablespoon oil in wok. Crack eggs into wok; cook and stir 45 seconds or until eggs are scrambled but still moist. Add chicken and vegetable mixture, rice, soy sauce and sesame seeds; cook and stir 2 minutes or until well blended and heated through. Season with additional salt and pepper.

MAKES 4 SERVINGS

CHINA

POT STICKERS

- 2 cups all-purpose flour
- ¾ cup plus 2 tablespoons boiling water
- ½ cup very finely chopped napa cabbage
- 8 ounces lean ground pork
- 2 tablespoons finely chopped water chestnuts
- 1 green onion, finely chopped
- 1½ teaspoons dry sherry
- 1½ teaspoons soy sauce
- 1½ teaspoons cornstarch
- ½ teaspoon minced fresh ginger
- ½ teaspoon dark sesame oil
- ¼ teaspoon sugar
- 2 tablespoons vegetable oil
- ⅔ cup chicken broth
  Soy sauce, vinegar and chili oil

1 Place 2 cups flour in large bowl; make well in center. Pour in boiling water; stir with wooden spoon until dough forms. Turn out dough onto lightly floured surface; knead about 5 minutes or until smooth and satiny. Cover and let rest 30 minutes.

2 Squeeze cabbage to remove as much moisture as possible; place in large bowl. Stir in pork, water chestnuts, green onion, sherry, soy sauce, cornstarch, ginger, sesame oil and sugar.

3 Divide dough in half; cover one half with plastic wrap or clean towel while working with other half. Roll out dough to ⅛-inch thickness on lightly floured surface. Cut out 3-inch circles with round cookie cutter or top of clean empty can.

4 Place 1 rounded teaspoonful pork mixture in center of each dough circle. Lightly moisten edges of one dough circle with water; fold in half. Starting at one end, pinch edges together making four pleats along edge; set pot sticker down firmly, seam side up. Cover finished pot stickers while shaping remaining pot stickers. (Pot stickers may be refrigerated up to 4 hours or frozen in large resealable food storage bag.)

5 Heat 1 tablespoon vegetable oil in large nonstick skillet over medium heat. Place half of pot stickers in skillet, seam side up. (If cooking frozen pot stickers, do not thaw.) Cook 5 to 6 minutes or until bottoms are golden brown.

6 Pour in ⅓ cup broth; cover tightly. Reduce heat to low; cook about 10 minutes or until all liquid is absorbed (15 minutes if frozen). Repeat with remaining vegetable oil, pot stickers and broth. Serve with soy sauce, vinegar and chili oil for dipping.

MAKES ABOUT 3 DOZEN POT STICKERS

TONKATSU
(BREADED PORK CUTLETS)

Tonkatsu Sauce
(recipe follows)
1 pound pork tenderloin,
trimmed
Salt and black pepper
½ cup all-purpose flour
2 eggs
2 tablespoons water
1½ cups panko bread crumbs
6 to 8 tablespoons
vegetable oil, divided
Hot cooked rice

1 Prepare Tonkatsu Sauce; set aside.

2 Cut pork diagonally into ½-inch-thick slices; season with salt and pepper. Spread flour on medium plate. Beat eggs and water in shallow bowl. Spread panko on another medium plate. Dip each pork slice first in flour, then egg. Shake off excess, then coat pork with panko.

3 Heat 2 tablespoons oil in large nonstick skillet over medium heat. Add as many pork cutlets as can fit without overlapping; do not crowd skillet. Cook over medium heat 4 minutes per side or until cooked thorough. Remove pork to paper towel-lined plate to drain; tent with foil to keep warm. Repeat with remaining pork, adding additional oil as necessary.

4 Serve over rice with Tonkatsu Sauce.

MAKES 4 SERVINGS

TONKATSU SAUCE

¼ cup ketchup
1 tablespoon soy sauce
2 teaspoons sugar
2 teaspoons mirin (Japanese
sweet rice wine)
1 teaspoon Worcestershire
sauce
½ teaspoon grated
fresh ginger
1 clove garlic, minced

Combine ketchup, soy sauce, sugar, mirin, Worcestershire sauce, ginger and garlic in small bowl; mix well.

MAKES ABOUT ⅓ CUP

PRESSURE COOKER BUTTER CHICKEN

2 tablespoons butter

1 onion, chopped

4 cloves garlic, minced

1 teaspoon minced fresh ginger

1 teaspoon ground turmeric

1 teaspoon ground coriander

1 teaspoon garam masala

1 teaspoon ground cumin

½ teaspoon ground red pepper

½ teaspoon paprika

1 can (about 14 ounces) diced tomatoes

¾ teaspoon salt

2 pounds boneless skinless chicken breasts, cut into 2-inch pieces

½ cup whipping cream

Chopped fresh cilantro

Hot cooked rice (optional)

1 Press Sauté on electric pressure cooker; melt butter in pot. Add onion; cook and stir about 4 minutes or until onion begins to turn golden. Add garlic and ginger; cook and stir 1 minute. Add turmeric, coriander, garam masala, cumin, red pepper and paprika; cook and stir 30 seconds. Add tomatoes and salt; cook and stir 2 minutes. Stir in chicken; mix well.

2 Secure lid and move pressure release valve to sealing or locked position. Cook at high pressure 8 minutes.

3 When cooking is complete, use natural release for 10 minutes, then release remaining pressure.

4 Press Sauté; adjust heat to low. Stir in cream; cook 5 minutes or until heated through. Sprinkle with cilantro; serve with rice, if desired.

MAKES 4 TO 6 SERVINGS

Note

To make this dish on the stovetop, melt butter in large saucepan over medium-high heat; proceed with step 1. Reduce heat to medium-low; simmer 15 to 20 minutes or until chicken is cooked through, stirring occasionally. Stir in cream; cook 5 minutes or until heated through and sauce is slightly thickened.

CELLOPHANE NOODLES WITH MINCED PORK

1 package (about 4 ounces) cellophane noodles*

32 dried shiitake mushrooms

2 tablespoons minced fresh ginger

2 tablespoons black bean sauce

1½ cups chicken broth

1 tablespoon dry sherry

1 tablespoon soy sauce

2 tablespoons vegetable oil

6 ounces lean ground pork

3 green onions, sliced

1 jalapeño or other hot pepper, seeded and finely chopped

Fresh cilantro sprigs and hot red peppers (optional)

Cellophane noodles (also called bean threads or glass noodles) are thin, translucent noodles sold in tangled bunches.

1 Place cellophane noodles and dried mushrooms in separate medium bowls; cover each with hot water. Let stand 30 minutes; drain.

2 Cut cellophane noodles into 4-inch pieces. Squeeze out excess water from mushrooms. Cut off and discard mushroom stems; cut caps into thin slices.

3 Combine ginger and black bean sauce in small bowl. Combine broth, sherry and soy sauce in medium bowl.

4 Heat oil in wok or large skillet over high heat. Add pork; stir-fry 2 minutes or until no longer pink. Add green onions, jalapeño pepper and black bean sauce mixture; stir-fry 1 minute.

5 Add broth mixture, noodles and mushrooms to wok; cook over medium heat about 5 minutes or until most of liquid is absorbed. Garnish with cilantro and red peppers.

MAKES 4 SERVINGS

JAPAN

JAPANESE–STYLE SIMMERED CHICKEN THIGHS

3 medium carrots, peeled and cut into 2-inch pieces

8 ounces shiitake mushrooms, stemmed and quarted

1 medium onion, cut into 1-inch pieces

1 medium Japanese eggplant, halved lengthwise and cut into ½-inch-thick slices

2 pounds boneless skinless chicken thighs

½ cup tamari or reduced-sodium soy sauce

⅓ cup chicken broth

½ cup sugar

¼ cup mirin (Japanese sweet rice wine)

1 tablespoon cornstarch

1 teaspoon grated fresh ginger

1 teaspoon minced garlic

1 whole star anise*

1 tablespoon sesame seeds, toasted

Hot cooked rice (optional)

Or substitute ¼ teaspoon Chinese five-spice powder.

Slow Cooker Directions

1 Combine carrots, mushrooms, onion and eggplant in slow cooker; top with chicken thighs.

2 Combine soy sauce, broth, sugar, mirin, cornstarch, ginger, garlic and star anise in small saucepan; bring to simmer over medium heat. Cook until sugar dissolves and mixture thickens slightly, stirring occasionally. Pour over chicken and vegetables.

3 Cover and cook on LOW 7 hours or until chicken and vegetables are tender.

4 Remove and discard star anise. Stir in sesame seeds. Serve with rice, if desired.

MAKES 6 TO 8 SERVINGS

THAILAND

PAD THAI
(THAI FRIED NOODLES)

7¼ cups water, divided

12 ounces dried thin rice
  stick noodles

4 tablespoons vegetable oil,
  divided

3 tablespoons packed
  brown sugar

3 tablespoons soy sauce

2 tablespoons lime juice

1 tablespoon anchovy paste
  or fish sauce

2 eggs, lightly beaten

12 ounces medium shrimp,
  peeled and deveined

2 cloves garlic, minced

1 tablespoon paprika

¼ to ½ teaspoon ground
  red pepper

1 red bell pepper, thinly
  sliced (optional)

6 ounces fresh bean sprouts
  (optional)

½ cup coarsely chopped
  unsalted dry-roasted
  peanuts

4 green onions, sliced

¼ cup shredded carrot
  (optional)

  Lime wedges

1 Place 6 cups water in wok; bring to a boil over high heat. Add noodles; cook 2 minutes or until tender but still firm, stirring frequently. Drain and rinse under cold water to stop cooking. Drain again and place noodles in large bowl. Add 1 tablespoon oil; toss lightly to coat. Set aside.

2 Combine remaining 1¼ cups water, brown sugar, soy sauce, lime juice and anchovy paste in small bowl; mix well.

3 Heat wok over medium heat about 30 seconds or until hot. Drizzle 1 tablespoon oil into wok and heat 15 seconds. Add eggs; cook 1 minute or just until set on bottom. Turn eggs over; stir to scramble until cooked but not dry. Transfer to medium bowl.

4 Heat wok over high heat until hot. Drizzle 1 tablespoon oil into wok; heat 15 seconds. Add shrimp and garlic; stir-fry 2 minutes or until shrimp begin to turn pink and opaque. Add shrimp to bowl with eggs.

5 Heat wok over medium heat until hot. Drizzle remaining 1 tablespoon oil into wok; heat 15 seconds. Stir in paprika and red pepper. Add cooked noodles, soy sauce mixture and bell pepper, if desired; cook and stir about 5 minutes or until noodles are softened. Stir in bean sprouts, if desired. Add peanuts and green onions; cook and stir about 1 minute or until green onions begin to wilt.

6 Return eggs and shrimp to wok with carrot, if desired; cook and stir until heated through. Transfer to serving plate; serve with lime wedges.

MAKES 4 SERVINGS

KOREAN BEEF SHORT RIBS

2½ pounds beef chuck
   flanken-style short ribs,
   cut ⅜ to ½ inch thick*

¼ cup chopped green onions

¼ cup water

¼ cup soy sauce

1 tablespoon sugar

2 teaspoons grated fresh
   ginger

2 teaspoons dark
   sesame oil

2 cloves garlic, minced

½ teaspoon black pepper

1 tablespoon sesame seeds,
   toasted*

*Flanken-style ribs can be
ordered from your butcher.
They are cross-cut short ribs
sawed through the bones.*

**To toast sesame seeds, spread
seeds in small skillet. Shake
skillet over medium-low heat
3 minutes or until seeds begin
to pop and turn golden.*

1 Place ribs in large resealable food storage bag. Combine green onions, water, soy sauce, sugar, ginger, oil, garlic and pepper in small bowl; pour over ribs. Seal bag; turn to coat. Marinate in refrigerator at least 4 hours or up to 8 hours, turning occasionally.

2 Prepare grill for direct cooking over medium-high heat. Remove ribs from marinade; reserve marinade.

3 Grill ribs, covered, 5 minutes. Brush lightly with reserved marinade; turn and brush again. Discard remaining marinade. Grill, covered, 5 to 6 minutes for medium (165°F) or to desired doneness. Sprinkle with sesame seeds.

MAKES 4 TO 6 SERVINGS

KUNG PAO CHICKEN

5 teaspoons dry sherry, divided

5 teaspoons soy sauce, divided

3½ teaspoons cornstarch, divided

¼ teaspoon salt

3 boneless skinless chicken breasts (about 1 pound), cut into bite-size pieces

2 tablespoons chicken broth or water

1 tablespoon red wine vinegar

1½ teaspoons sugar

3 tablespoons vegetable oil, divided

⅓ cup salted peanuts

6 to 8 small dried red chiles

1½ teaspoons minced fresh ginger

2 green onions, cut into 1½-inch pieces

1 Combine 2 teaspoons sherry, 2 teaspoons soy sauce, 2 teaspoons cornstarch and salt in large bowl; mix well. Add chicken; stir to coat. Let stand 30 minutes.

2 Combine remaining 3 teaspoons sherry, 3 teaspoons soy sauce, 1½ teaspoons cornstarch, broth, vinegar and sugar in small bowl; mix well.

3 Heat 1 tablespoon oil in wok or large skillet over medium heat. Add peanuts; stir-fry until lightly toasted. Remove to plate. Heat remaining 2 tablespoons oil in wok over medium heat. Add chiles; stir-fry 1 minute or just until chiles begin to char.

4 Increase heat to high. Add chicken mixture; stir-fry 2 minutes. Add ginger; stir-fry 1 minute or until chicken is cooked through. Stir in peanuts and green onions. Stir cornstarch mixture; add to wok. Cook and stir until sauce boils and thickens.

MAKES 3 SERVINGS

VEGETARIAN SUSHI

1¼ cups Japanese short grain sushi rice*

1½ cups water

1 teaspoon dark sesame oil

4 medium shiitake mushrooms, thinly sliced

4 thin asparagus spears

2½ tablespoons seasoned rice vinegar

3 sheets nori (from 0.6-ounce package)

Prepared wasabi

½ red bell pepper, cut into very thin strips

½ unpeeled seedless cucumber, cut into long thin slivers

Pickled ginger and soy sauce

If you can't find white rice labeled "sushi rice", use any short grain rice.

1 Rinse rice in several changes of water to remove excess starch; drain. Combine rice and 1½ cups water in medium saucepan; bring to a boil over high heat. Reduce heat to very low; cover and cook 15 to 20 minutes or until rice is tender and liquid is absorbed. Let stand, covered, 10 minutes.

2 Meanwhile, heat oil in small nonstick skillet over medium heat. Add mushrooms; cook and stir 2 to 3 minutes or until tender. Wrap asparagus in plastic wrap; microwave on HIGH 1 minute to blanch.

3 Spoon warm rice into shallow nonmetallic bowl. Sprinkle vinegar over rice; fold in gently with wooden spoon. Cut nori sheet in half lengthwise, parallel to lines marked on rough side. Place lengthwise, shiny side down, on bamboo rolling mat about three slats from edge nearest to you.

4 Prepare small bowl with water and splash of vinegar to rinse fingers and prevent rice from sticking while working. Spread about ½ cup rice over nori, leaving ½-inch border at top edge. Spread pinch of wasabi across center of rice. Arrange strips of two different vegetable fillings over wasabi; do not overfill.

5 Pick up edge of mat nearest you. Roll mat forward, wrapping rice around fillings and pressing gently to form log. Once roll is formed, press gently to seal; place completed roll on cutting board, seam side down. Repeat with remaining nori and fillings.

6 Slice each roll into six pieces with sharp knife, wiping knife with damp cloth between cuts. Serve with pickled ginger, soy sauce and additional wasabi for dipping.

MAKES 36 PIECES (6 ROLLS)

BASIL CHICKEN WITH RICE NOODLES

1 pound boneless skinless chicken breasts, cut into bite-size pieces

5 tablespoons soy sauce, divided

1 tablespoon white wine or rice wine (optional)

3 cloves garlic, minced

1 tablespoon grated fresh ginger

8 ounces uncooked rice noodles

1 red onion, sliced

1 yellow or red bell pepper, cut into strips

2 medium carrots, cut into matchstick-size pieces

2 jalapeño or serrano peppers, seeded and chopped

Juice of 2 limes

2 tablespoons packed brown sugar

1 tablespoon vegetable oil

1½ cups loosely packed fresh basil leaves, shredded

1 Place chicken in shallow dish. Combine 3 tablespoons soy sauce, wine, if desired, garlic and ginger in small bowl; mix well. Pour over chicken; stir to coat. Marinate at room temperature 30 minutes or refrigerate up to 2 hours.

2 Place noodles in large bowl. Cover with hot water; let stand 15 minutes or until tender. Drain.

3 Combine onion, bell pepper, carrots and jalapeño peppers in medium bowl. Whisk remaining 2 tablespoons soy sauce, lime juice and brown sugar in small bowl until sugar is dissolved.

4 Heat oil in wok or large skillet over medium-high heat. Add chicken with marinade; stir-fry 5 minutes or until cooked through. Add vegetables; stir-fry 4 to 6 minutes or until crisp-tender.

5 Stir lime juice mixture and add to wok; cook and stir 2 minutes. Add noodles and basil; toss to combine.

MAKES 4 SERVINGS

JAPAN

OKONOMIYAKI (SAVORY PANCAKE)

1 cup all-purpose flour

2 eggs

½ teaspoon salt

1 cup finely chopped cabbage

2 green onions, chopped

¾ to 1 cup water

Assorted fillings: cooked chicken or beef, cubed tofu, sliced red bell pepper, asparagus, corn and/or mushrooms

4 teaspoons vegetable oil

Sauce

¼ cup ketchup

2 tablespoons sake

1½ tablespoons Worcestershire sauce

1 teaspoon tamari or soy sauce

¼ teaspoon Dijon mustard

Mayonnaise (optional)

1 Whisk flour, eggs and salt in medium bowl until combined. (Some lumps are fine.) Stir in cabbage, green onions and ¾ cup water. Add enough additional water to make batter the consistency of thick pancake batter.

2 Prepare fillings. (You will need about ⅓ cup of mixed fillings for each pancake.)

3 Heat large nonstick skillet or griddle over medium-high heat. Brush skillet with 1 teaspoon oil; ladle in one fourth of batter and spread into circle. Cook 2 minutes; arrange fillings on top and press gently into batter with spatula. Cook 2 to 3 minutes or until edges of pancake look dull and underside is lightly browned. Turn pancake and continue cooking 2 to 4 minutes or until cooked through. Remove to platter; keep warm. Repeat with remaining oil, batter and fillings.

4 Meanwhile for sauce, combine ketchup, sake, Worcestershire sauce, tamari and mustard in small saucepan; cook over medium-low heat 1 minute, stirring constantly. Let cool to room temperature.

5 Drizzle okonomiyaki with sauce; serve with mayonnaise, if desired.

MAKES 4 SERVINGS

Tip

Okonomiyaki is a favorite Japanese snack food, enjoyed in bars and quick-serve restaurants like pizza. Choose whatever fillings you like and have on hand; anything from seaweed to roast beef can be used.

SZECHUAN BEEF LO MEIN

1 boneless beef top sirloin
steak (about 1 pound)

4 cloves garlic, minced

2 teaspoons minced
fresh ginger

¾ teaspoon red pepper
flakes, divided

1 tablespoon vegetable oil

1 can (about 14 ounces)
vegetable broth

1 cup water

2 tablespoons reduced-
sodium soy sauce

1 package (8 ounces)
frozen mixed vegetables
for stir-fry

1 package (9 ounces)
refrigerated angel
hair pasta *or* 8 ounces
dried angel hair pasta

¼ cup chopped fresh
cilantro (optional)

1 Cut beef in half lengthwise, then cut crosswise
into thin slices. Combine beef, garlic, ginger and
½ teaspoon red pepper flakes in medium bowl;
mix well.

2 Heat oil in wok or large nonstick skillet over
medium-high heat. Add half of beef; stir-fry
2 minutes or until meat is barely pink in center.
Remove to plate. Repeat with remaining beef.

3 Add broth, water, soy sauce and remaining
¼ teaspoon red pepper flakes to wok; bring
to a boil over high heat. Add vegetables; return
to a boil. Reduce heat to low; cover and simmer
3 minutes or until vegetables are crisp-tender.

4 Stir in pasta; return to a boil over high heat.
Reduce heat to medium; cook, uncovered,
2 minutes, separating pasta with two forks.
Return beef and any accumulated juices to
wok; cook 1 minute or until pasta is tender
and beef is heated through. Sprinkle with
cilantro, if desired.

MAKES 4 SERVINGS

NAAN (INDIAN FLATBREAD)

1 package (¼ ounce) active dry yeast

1 teaspoon sugar

¼ cup plus 2 tablespoons warm water (105° to 115°F), divided

3 cups all-purpose flour

1 teaspoon salt

1 teaspoon kalonji* seeds or poppy seeds (optional)

½ cup plain whole milk Greek yogurt

¼ cup (½ stick) melted butter, plus additional butter for brushing on naan

Kalonji seed is often called onion seed or black cumin seed. It is available in Indian markets and is traditional in some varieties of naan.

1 Dissolve yeast and sugar in 2 tablespoons warm water in small bowl; let stand 5 minutes or until bubbly. Combine flour, salt and kalonji, if desired, in large bowl of stand mixer.

2 Add yeast mixture, yogurt and ¼ cup butter; mix with dough hook at low speed until blended. Add remaining ¼ cup water, 1 tablespoon at a time, until dough comes together and cleans side of bowl. (You may not need all the water.) Mix at low speed 5 to 7 minutes or until dough is smooth and elastic.

3 Shape dough into a ball. Place dough in greased bowl; turn to grease top. Cover and let rise in warm place 1½ to 2 hours or until doubled in size.

4 Punch down dough. Divide dough into six pieces; roll each piece into a ball. Place on plate sprayed with nonstick cooking spray; cover and let rest 10 to 15 minutes.

5 Meanwhile, prepare grill for direct cooking or preheat oven to 500°F with baking stone on rack in lower third of oven. (Remove other racks.)

6 Place each ball of dough on lightly floured surface; roll and stretch into ⅛-inch-thick oval. Place on grill or baking stone two or three at a time. Grill, covered, or bake 2 minutes until puffed. Turn, brush tops with butter and grill or bake 1 to 2 minutes or until browned in patches on both sides. Brush bottoms with butter. Cut in half, if desired; serve warm.

MAKES 6 TO 12 SERVINGS

MUSHROOM AND KALE SLICE

4 ounces cremini mushrooms, stems trimmed, cut into thirds

1 tablespoon olive oil, divided

½ teaspoon plus ⅛ teaspoon salt, divided

½ cup chopped onion

1 cup packed chopped stemmed lacinato kale

½ cup halved grape tomatoes

4 eggs

½ teaspoon Italian seasoning

Black pepper

⅓ cup shredded mozzarella cheese

1 tablespoon shredded Parmesan cheese

Chopped fresh parsley (optional)

1 Preheat oven to 400°F. Spread mushrooms on small baking sheet; drizzle with 1 teaspoon oil and sprinkle with ⅛ teaspoon salt. Roast 15 to 20 minutes or until well browned and tender.

2 Heat remaining 2 teaspoons oil in small (6- to 8-inch) ovenproof nonstick skillet over medium heat. Add onion; cook and stir 5 minutes or until soft. Add kale and ¼ teaspoon salt; cook and stir 10 minutes or until kale is tender. Add tomatoes; cook and stir 3 minutes or until tomatoes are soft. Stir in mushrooms.

3 Preheat broiler. Whisk eggs, remaining ¼ teaspoon salt, Italian seasoning and pepper in small bowl until well blended.

4 Pour egg mixture over vegetables in skillet; stir gently to mix. Cook 3 minutes or until eggs are set around edge, lifting edge to allow uncooked portion to flow underneath. Sprinkle with mozzarella and Parmesan.

5 Broil 3 minutes or until eggs are set and cheese is browned. Cut into wedges; garnish with parsley.

MAKES 2 SERVINGS

 *Australia*

SAUSAGE ROLLS

8 ounces lean ground pork

¼ cup finely chopped onion

½ teaspoon coarse salt

1 teaspoon minced garlic

½ teaspoon dried thyme

½ teaspoon dried basil

¼ teaspoon dried marjoram

¼ teaspoon black pepper

1 sheet frozen puff pastry (half of 17-ounce package), thawed

1 egg, beaten

1 Preheat oven to 400°F. Line large baking sheet with parchment paper.

2 Combine pork, onion, salt, garlic, thyme, basil, marjoram and pepper in medium bowl; mix well.

3 Place puff pastry on floured surface; cut lengthwise into three strips at seams. Roll each third into 10×4½-inch rectangle. Shape one third of pork mixture into 10-inch log; arrange log along top edge of one pastry rectangle. Brush bottom ½ inch of rectangle with egg. Roll pastry down around pork; press to seal. Cut each roll crosswise into four pieces; place seam side down on prepared baking sheet. Repeat with remaining puff pastry and pork mixture. Brush top of each roll with egg.

4 Bake about 25 minutes or until sausage is cooked through and pastry is golden brown and puffed. Remove to wire rack to cool 10 minutes. Serve warm.

MAKES 4 SERVINGS

BRAISED LAMB SHANKS

- 2 tablespoons all-purpose flour
- 1 teaspoon salt
- ½ teaspoon ground black pepper
- 4 lamb shanks (4 to 5 pounds total)
- 2 to 3 tablespoons olive oil
- 1 tablespoon butter
- 1 large onion, chopped
- 4 cloves garlic, minced
- 1 cup beef or chicken broth
- 1 cup dry red wine
- 2 tablespoons chopped fresh rosemary leaves *or* 2 teaspoons dried rosemary

1 Combine flour, salt and pepper in large resealable food storage bag. Add lamb shanks, one at a time, to bag; shake to coat lightly with seasoned flour. (Use all of flour mixture.)

2 Heat 2 tablespoons oil and butter in Dutch oven over medium heat. Add lamb shanks in batches; cook until browned on all sides. Remove to plate.

3 Add remaining 1 tablespoon oil to Dutch oven, if needed. Add onion and garlic; cook 5 minutes, scraping up browned bits from bottom of pan. Add broth, wine and rosemary; bring to a boil over high heat.

4 Return lamb and any accumulated juices to Dutch oven. Reduce heat to low; cover and simmer 1½ to 2 hours or until lamb is fork-tender. Remove lamb to serving platter; cover loosely to keep warm.

5 Skim off and discard fat from liquid in Dutch oven. Boil liquid until reduced to 2 cups and slightly thickened. (Depending on amount of remaining liquid, this could take from 2 to 10 minutes.) Pour sauce over lamb.

MAKES 4 SERVINGS

TANGY BARBECUED LAMB

¾ cup chili sauce

½ cup beer (not light beer)

½ cup honey

¼ cup reduced-sodium Worcestershire sauce

¼ cup finely chopped onion

2 cloves garlic, minced

½ teaspoon red pepper flakes

¼ teaspoon sea salt

5 pounds lamb ribs, well trimmed and cut into individual ribs

1 Combine chili sauce, beer, honey, Worcestershire sauce, onion, garlic, red pepper flakes and salt in small saucepan; bring to a boil over high heat. Reduce heat to low; cover and simmer 10 minutes. Remove from heat; cool to room temperature.

2 Place lamb in large resealable food storage bag; pour chili mixture over lamb. Seal bag; turn to coat. Marinate in refrigerator at least 2 hours, turning occasionally.

3 Prepare grill for indirect cooking over medium heat (see Tip). Oil grid.

4 Remove lamb from marinade; reserve marinade. Place lamb on grid over drip pan. Grill, covered, 45 minutes or until lamb is tender, turning and brushing with marinade every 15 minutes. Place remaining marinade in small saucepan and bring to a boil; boil 1 minute. Serve with lamb.

MAKES 6 SERVINGS

Tip

To set up gas grill for indirect cooking, preheat all burners on high. Turn one burner off; place food over "off" burner. Reset remaining burner(s) to medium; close lid to cook. To set up charcoal grill for indirect cooking, arrange hot coals around outer edge of grill; place disposable foil pan in open space. Place food over open area and close lid to cook.

MARINATED GRILLED LAMB CHOPS

8 well-trimmed lamb loin
   chops, 1 inch thick
   (4 to 5 ounces each)

3 cloves garlic, minced

2 tablespoons chopped
   fresh rosemary leaves
   or 2 teaspoons dried
   rosemary

2 tablespoons chopped
   fresh mint *or*
   2 teaspoons dried mint

¾ cup dry red wine

⅓ cup butter, softened

¼ teaspoon salt

¼ teaspoon black pepper

   Fresh mint leaves
   (optional)

1 Place lamb in large resealable food storage bag. Combine garlic, rosemary and chopped mint in small bowl; mix well. Combine half of garlic mixture and wine in glass measuring cup; pour mixture over lamb. Seal bag; turn to coat. Marinate in refrigerator at least 2 hours or up to 4 hours, turning occasionally.

2 Add butter, salt and pepper to remaining garlic mixture; stir until well blended. Spoon onto center of sheet of plastic wrap. Shape butter mixture into 4×1½-inch log; wrap securely in plastic wrap. Refrigerate until ready to serve.

3 Prepare grill for direct cooking over medium heat. Drain lamb, discarding marinade.

4 Grill lamb, covered, 4 to 5 minutes per side or until 160°F for medium or until desired doneness.

5 Cut butter log crosswise into eight ½-inch slices. Top each lamb chop with butter slice. Garnish with mint leaves.

MAKES 4 SERVINGS

COCONUT SCONES
WITH ORANGE BUTTER

1¾ cups all-purpose flour

½ teaspoon salt

1 tablespoon baking
    powder

2 tablespoons sugar

5 tablespoons cold butter,
    cut into small pieces

1 egg

1 cup whipping cream,
    divided

2 tablespoons milk

2 teaspoons grated orange
    peel

½ cup plus ⅓ cup sweetened
    flaked coconut, divided

   Orange Butter (recipe
    follows, optional)

1 Preheat oven to 400°F. Line baking sheet with
   parchment paper.

2 Combine flour, salt, baking powder and sugar in
   large bowl; mix well. Cut in butter with pastry
   blender or two knives until mixture resembles
   coarse crumbs. Whisk egg, ¾ cup cream, milk,
   orange peel and ½ cup coconut in medium bowl
   until blended. Add to flour mixture; stir just until
   dough forms.

3 Turn out dough onto lightly floured surface; pat
   into 8-inch circle about ¾-inch thick. Cut into
   eight wedges. Brush tops with remaining ¼ cup
   cream; sprinkle with remaining ⅓ cup coconut.
   Place 2 inches apart on prepared baking sheet.

4 Bake 12 to 15 minutes or until golden brown and
   coconut is toasted. Remove to wire rack to cool
   15 minutes. Prepare Orange Butter, if desired.
   Serve with warm scones.

MAKES 8 SCONES

ORANGE BUTTER

½ cup (1 stick) butter,
    softened

2 tablespoons orange juice

1 tablespoon grated
    orange peel

2 teaspoons sugar

Combine butter, orange juice, orange peel and
sugar in medium bowl; beat with electric mixer
at low speed until well blended and creamy.

MAKES ABOUT 1 CUP

AUSTRALIAN DAMPER BREAD

3 cups self-rising flour

1 teaspoon salt

6 tablespoons (¾ stick) cold butter, cut into pieces

1½ cups milk

1 Preheat oven to 375°F. Line 9-inch cast iron skillet or baking sheet with parchment paper.

2 Whisk flour and salt in medium bowl. Add butter; mix with fingers, squeezing butter into flour until coarse crumbs form. Stir in milk until dough forms.

3 Turn out dough onto floured surface; pat into 9-inch circle with floured or dampened hands. Place dough in prepared skillet; score deep X shape into top with sharp knife.

4 Bake 25 to 30 minutes or until top is lightly browned and toothpick inserted into center comes out clean.

MAKES 6 TO 8 SERVINGS

BROCCOLI AND CHEDDAR SCONES

2½ cups all-purpose flour

1 tablespoon baking powder

1 tablespoon sugar

2 teaspoons salt

½ teaspoon red pepper flakes

1 cup broccoli florets

½ cup (1 stick) cold butter, cut into small pieces

1½ cups (6 ounces) shredded Cheddar cheese

1 cup milk

1 Preheat oven to 400°F. Line baking sheets with parchment paper.

2 Combine flour, baking powder, sugar, salt and red pepper flakes in food processor; process 10 seconds. Add broccoli and butter; process until mixture forms coarse meal, scraping down side of bowl once. Transfer mixture to large bowl. Add cheese and milk; stir until blended. Knead gently to form dough.

3 Divide dough in half. Press one half of dough into 8-inch circle. Cut into eight wedges; place on prepared baking sheet. Repeat with remaining half of dough.

4 Bake 15 to 20 minutes or until lightly browned.

MAKES 16 SCONES

PAVLOVA

Meringue Shell

- 4 extra-large egg whites, at room temperature
- ¼ teaspoon cream of tartar
- 1 cup sugar
- 1 tablespoon plus 1 teaspoon cornstarch, sifted
- ½ teaspoon white vinegar
- ½ teaspoon vanilla

Filling

- 1 cup whipping cream
- 1 tablespoon sugar
- 2 teaspoons vanilla

Assembly

- ½ cup sliced fresh strawberries
- ½ cup raspberries, blackberries or blueberries
- 1 kiwi, peeled and thinly sliced

1 Position rack in center of oven; preheat oven to 400°F. Line baking sheet with foil. Using 9-inch cake pan as a guide, trace 9-inch circle onto dull side of foil with pencil, then turn foil over on baking sheet.

2 Combine egg whites and cream of tartar in medium bowl of stand mixer; whip with wire whip attachment at medium speed until foamy. Gradually add 1 cup sugar, beating about 3 minutes or until egg whites hold glossy and firm, but not stiff, peaks. Sprinkle with cornstarch, vinegar and vanilla; fold in gently with rubber spatula.

3 Use rubber spatula to spread meringue mixture on foil circle. Mound mixture around edges so edges are slightly thicker than center, creating shallow bowl. Place baking sheet in oven. *Reduce oven temperature to 250°F;* bake meringue 1½ hours.

4 Turn off oven and prop open oven door with wooden spoon. Leave meringue in oven until cool. Remove baking sheet from oven; carefully peel foil off back of meringue. Place meringue on serving plate. (Meringue shell can be made up to 2 days in advance. Store at room temperature tightly wrapped in foil.)

5 Place cream bowl of stand mixer; whip at high speed 1 to 2 minutes or until soft peaks form. Gradually add 1 tablespoon sugar and 2 teaspoons vanilla; whip until stiff peaks form.

6 Spread whipped cream over center of meringue shell. Arrange fruit over whipped cream. Refrigerate until ready to serve (no more than 3 hours).

MAKES 8 TO 10 SERVINGS

METRIC CONVERSION CHART

VOLUME MEASUREMENTS (dry)

$1/8$ teaspoon = 0.5 mL
$1/4$ teaspoon = 1 mL
$1/2$ teaspoon = 2 mL
$3/4$ teaspoon = 4 mL
1 teaspoon = 5 mL
1 tablespoon = 15 mL
2 tablespoons = 30 mL
$1/4$ cup = 60 mL
$1/3$ cup = 75 mL
$1/2$ cup = 125 mL
$2/3$ cup = 150 mL
$3/4$ cup = 175 mL
1 cup = 250 mL
2 cups = 1 pint = 500 mL
3 cups = 750 mL
4 cups = 1 quart = 1 L

VOLUME MEASUREMENTS (fluid)

1 fluid ounce (2 tablespoons) = 30 mL
4 fluid ounces ($1/2$ cup) = 125 mL
8 fluid ounces (1 cup) = 250 mL
12 fluid ounces ($1\frac{1}{2}$ cups) = 375 mL
16 fluid ounces (2 cups) = 500 mL

WEIGHTS (mass)

$1/2$ ounce = 15 g
1 ounce = 30 g
3 ounces = 90 g
4 ounces = 120 g
8 ounces = 225 g
10 ounces = 285 g
12 ounces = 360 g
16 ounces = 1 pound = 450 g

DIMENSIONS

$1/16$ inch = 2 mm
$1/8$ inch = 3 mm
$1/4$ inch = 6 mm
$1/2$ inch = 1.5 cm
$3/4$ inch = 2 cm
1 inch = 2.5 cm

OVEN TEMPERATURES

250°F = 120°C
275°F = 140°C
300°F = 150°C
325°F = 160°C
350°F = 180°C
375°F = 190°C
400°F = 200°C
425°F = 220°C
450°F = 230°C

BAKING PAN SIZES

Utensil	Size in Inches/Quarts	Metric Volume	Size in Centimeters
Baking or Cake Pan (square or rectangular)	$8 \times 8 \times 2$	2 L	$20 \times 20 \times 5$
	$9 \times 9 \times 2$	2.5 L	$23 \times 23 \times 5$
	$12 \times 8 \times 2$	3 L	$30 \times 20 \times 5$
	$13 \times 9 \times 2$	3.5 L	$33 \times 23 \times 5$
Loaf Pan	$8 \times 4 \times 3$	1.5 L	$20 \times 10 \times 7$
	$9 \times 5 \times 3$	2 L	$23 \times 13 \times 7$
Round Layer Cake Pan	$8 \times 1\frac{1}{2}$	1.2 L	20×4
	$9 \times 1\frac{1}{2}$	1.5 L	23×4
Pie Plate	$8 \times 1\frac{1}{4}$	750 mL	20×3
	$9 \times 1\frac{1}{4}$	1 L	23×3
Baking Dish or Casserole	1 quart	1 L	—
	$1\frac{1}{2}$ quart	1.5 L	—
	2 quart	2 L	—